PRAISE FOR

A Stranger at My Door

Propelled by profound acts of compassion and humanity, this story asks readers to reevaluate their notion of what it means to live an ethical life in America's borderlands. In it, Bowden collapses the distance that insulates her from the "other" and inspires us to do the same.

Francisco Cantú, author of
The Line Becomes a River: Dispatches from the Border

In a world obsessed with anger and hatred, Peg Bowden is a beam of light and love for all mankind. Truly welcoming the stranger, opening her heart and her home to those who are suffering, no one would ever be a stranger at Peg Bowden's door.

Shura Wallin, Co-founder
Green Valley/Sahuarita Samaritans

A Stranger at My Door seems to me a classic encounter: a lost and desperate stranger appears at the door of a middle-class woman who trusts him and takes him in. By degrees we get to know this migrant, and his plight, as well as the concern of the Samaritan, Peg Bowden. The drama continues in time and in different landscapes and countries. This is a drama of generosity and unexpectedness, illustrating the rewards of compassion. Peg Bowden's is an especially important book for the times we live in, and for all time.

Paul Theroux, author of
On the Plain of Snakes: A Mexican Journey

Peg Bowden is a wonderful writer, and *A Stranger at My Door* is a stunning work. She knows what she's talking about, and she can walk you out into territory you might never forget.

Luis Alberto Urrea, author of *The Devil's Highway*

Peg Bowden writes the story of too many people in the desert borderlands: ranchers, residents, bird-watchers, hikers, humanitarian-aid volunteers, and Border Patrol agents. Each person has the startling and unique experience of encountering a border-crosser. Every encounter is a profound challenge to that individual's values, faith, fears, allegiances, anxieties, and very soul. Like every gifted writer, Peg invites the reader into her soul-searching encounter, agonizing decisions, guilt, and redemption. We all should be companions on this struggle for the soul of America.

John Fife, co-founder of the Sanctuary Movement (1982);
founding member of Samaritans and No More Deaths;
retired pastor of Southside Presbyterian Church, Tucson;
convicted felon

To my desert angels, the Green Valley/Sahuarita Samaritans

TABLE OF CONTENTS

AUTHOR'S NOTE

In writing this memoir, I've done my best to stick to the facts. That said, I did take narrative liberties with the story. Some names have been changed to safeguard people's privacy. A few events were modified and compressed in part to protect the individuals involved. My actions were not a part of the ongoing activities of the Green Valley/Sahuarita Samaritans or any other humanitarian aid organization. Conversations were recollected from extensive notes and years of phone calls with my migrant friend in Guatemala. Others present during the encounters in this book may have a totally different perspective of what happened. Memories are like that.

Some of the scenes may make sense only to the people who were present, and some of the events may make absolutely no sense at all. I'm still trying to figure out why I did what I did. And why I didn't do more.

INTRODUCTION

I LIVE IN a place where most people wouldn't set foot, and yet I am absolutely sure I belong in this place. My home is in Arizona, and the news out of southern Arizona is always bad. In spite of the endless political arguments about who should cross our borders, what to do about the illegal drugs, the paramilitary agents toting guns and patrolling the wall, and the steady march of migrants, I love living in the desert. There is a tranquil spirituality that feeds my soul. This place I call home is a living, breathing plunge into a world of magical realism.

There have been times when I have staggered out of the desert after a long hike, half delirious with parched throat and blistered feet, not sure of my name or where I was going. In this country, a person can freeze at night and bake at high noon on the same day. But then I climb into my waiting car, crank up the air conditioner, and guzzle life-saving clean water from a gallon jug kept cool in the trunk. I am a *gringa*, a privileged white woman, and I live in the borderlands near Nogales, a twin border city we call *Ambos Nogales* that sprawls on both sides of the U.S./Mexico boundary.

The desert pushes my limits. Scrambling up a rocky precipice and sitting on the hard edges of a granite slab is my idea of a good time. The desert is my sacred place—a place of pilgrimages, where people walk to find themselves, to look inward, to be alone, to be in silence. It is holy ground. And people die here searching for a better life. *El norte* is their promised land.

Maybe it's the sun, maybe it's the extremes, maybe it's the harsh beauty, but life is frequently surreal in the desert. Magic is afoot. Ravens follow me on my walks with the dogs at our ranch. They fly in pairs (lovers for life), and we talk back and forth. I have perfected my raven voice over the years, and we have conversations. *Caw! Caw!* Raven talk is easier than Spanish. No past tenses to worry about. We always speak in the present.

This is a story of borders and the people who cross them. In a state of helplessness, fury, and awe, I watch this drama play out when I see Border Patrol vehicles rounding up migrants at the side of the road near my home. Human suffering is on display every week at an aid station for migrants in Nogales, Sonora, Mexico where I volunteer.

There is also a bright side to my life living near the border. I revel in the unique richness of this place: the delicious food, the music, the traditions, and the gentle hospitality of Mexican friends. I live in a land of great beauty and great pain.

My life in Arizona feels like an improvisation, a lot like jazz. Dissonant, erratic, squawking, occasionally sublime. I don't predict what's going to happen to me next week or next year. When I improvise at the piano, often my fingers take me in directions that I can't explain. Sometimes it works. Sometimes the whole musical experiment crashes and burns. When things are cooking, my fingers precede my brain. Then there is magic. When I quit obsessing about plans gone awry, my life is magic—a miracle. Like good jazz. If I can hit that balance of working at it without working at it, I am gifted with a sweet ending.

Living in the borderlands has been an immersion into events and circumstances that are difficult to predict or explain. The composition of each day advances, the theme moves in fits and starts, and then stumbles into a new variation. Occasionally there is a chord of resolution, but more often the chord is fragile, hanging on by a thread. Sometimes there are sour notes. Inexplicable. Discordant.

Nevertheless, the beat goes on.

"In the bleak mid-winter
Frosty wind made moan;
Earth stood hard as iron,
Water like a stone;
Snow had fallen, snow on snow,
Snow on snow,
In the bleak mid-winter
Long ago.

What can I give Him,
Poor as I am?
If I were a Shepherd
I would bring a lamb;
If I were a Wise Man
I would do my part,
Yet what I can I give Him,
Give my heart."
In The Bleak Midwinter, Christmas carol based on
the poem by Christina Rosetti, 1872.

But no stranger had to spend the night in the street, for my door was
always open to the traveler.
Job 31:32

"How can a person live a moral life in a culture of death?"
Some of the Dead Are Still Breathing, Charles Bowden, 2009

PART I

El Desierto

ONE

The Longest Night

DECEMBER 21, 2013
The Winter Solstice

3 p.m.
Margarita

THE DOGS KEEP barking. Nonstop.

On a drizzly, bone-chilling December afternoon in the mountains of southern Arizona, Cassie and Arroya, our two shelter rescue dogs, are creating quite a ruckus. I ignore them. After all, they are dogs. They bark at stuff.

But they keep sounding their alarm.

Frustrated with the racket, I go outside into the frigid rain and try to shush the dogs. It's spitting snow, and the rain feels like icy needles on my face. Cassie, the self-appointed watchdog, is staring across the steep canyon at something that has grabbed her attention. She's part golden Lab, part mutt, and she's trembling, beside herself with excitement. With her special ranch bark—the bark that commands my attention—she directs my gaze.

Our house sits on the edge of a deep canyon that separates us from the cliff on the other side. The dogs have seen a figure, perhaps a man, covered in a shiny black, plastic-looking poncho. He is walking toward the cliff's edge, stumbling and lurching. The black garment appears to be a garbage bag flapping in the wind. There's a hole in it where his head pokes through. Carrying an agave stem as a walking stick, the man raises both arms and shouts something unintelligible. He looks like Moses coming out of the wilderness. Or Jesus coming out of the desert. Or Darth Vader paying a surprise visit to planet Earth. Hushing the dogs, I look at this strange figure faltering unsteadily through the wintry mist. He looks straight at me and raises his stick.

The man stops walking, falls to his knees, and lifts both arms to the heavens. "Help me, help me," he says. "I am lost. My heart ... it is dying."

I have no idea who this person is.

On this day in December, my tranquility is shattered.

This is the day I break the law. Me—a silver-haired grandmother with nary a speeding ticket. I ignore the rule of law without remorse or hesitation. Placing my rational, law-abiding self on the back burner, I plunge into the abyss of the unknown like a foolhardy adolescent, damning the consequences.

I feel clean. Purposeful. Decent. Human. And scared.

Those days of law-breaking were some of the most memorable of my life.

⇒ • ⇐

DECEMBER 21
Nine hours earlier

IN THE BEGINNING, there is barely light.

It is 6 a.m. With one eye open I squint to catch a glimpse of a new day. As I look toward the east window of our desert home, the first hint of the sun's rays offers a distant hope. Outside it's pitch black. Crystals of frost cling to the windows. The temperature is well below freezing, and the quiet is profound. The only sounds I hear are my own shallow breathing and an occasional soft snore from my sleeping husband, Lester. There are no chirping birds to punctuate the silence on this frigid morning. No wonder people call it the dead of winter.

An icy mist hangs over the surrounding San Cayetano Mountains like a veil of lace. Soon an ephemeral shawl of blue haze creeps and crawls, snaking through the foothills surrounding our home. Staying in bed, I watch for threads of morning light. It's too cold to get up.

Today is the winter solstice. Reluctantly, I lower my bare feet to the floor and step onto the chilly Mexican tile on this twenty-first day of December. Trying to feel how this solstice day is different, significant, I imagine the slow, imperceptible tipping of the Earth, our precious blue marble, reaching toward the light. I reach for my own light, the bedside lamp, and brace myself for the wattage. Blinded by the sudden illumination, I wonder why I have to get up at all.

As I gingerly step outside into the winter dawn, there is absolute still-ness. It's a day for thermal socks and fuzzy slippers. The desert air crack-les with last night's hard frost. The earth is frozen and crunches under my slippers in the early glow. Frost is everywhere. My eyes immediately well with tears from the freezing chill. Blue Christmas icicle lights dan-gling from the porch rafters sparkle in the early light.

This is the desert in all its extremes. Winter in southern Arizona is not a subtle shift in temperatures. Two days ago it was seventy degrees; today it is well below freezing. The earth beneath my feet has become a Siberian block of ice.

Standing here on the front porch, I think about the vulnerability of my body in the numbing desert temperature. It doesn't take much to succumb to nature's whims in December. A fragile time for me, winter is the season when I am emotionally naked and sensitive. I am flooded with memories.

═══► ● ◄═══

TO BE PERFECTLY honest, I get a little crazy every December. Forty years ago was the time of our firstborn child. She was a beauty and arrived during a stormy winter morning on a farm in Wimer, Oregon, a tiny rural hamlet. My first glimpse was of her lavender-blue nakedness as she emerged from my body, pinking up right away.

Today, as I look to the east on this frigid Arizona morning, the sky is becoming lavender-blue, the same color as my newborn baby's skin. My breath quickens. I'm transported back to that 1973 in Oregon.

During my pregnancy I had dreamed of rocking my baby in the warmth of a December fire, staring at her perfect face, her perfect fingers, and all ten little toes. Truth be told, our firstborn arrived with a critical birth anomaly requiring multiple surgeries. Her face and sweet body were flawless, but inside all that perfection, something just wasn't working. Her body could not sustain life. The first Christmas was a nightmare of hospitals and waiting rooms. While the rest of the world sang of peace on Earth, our baby's first weeks were spent in a plastic box—an incubator—where she endured tubes and needles and pain.

Ever since, December has been a tightrope of vulnerability: A slight misstep plunges me into restless nights and fears that I don't want to face—the fear of losing someone you love more than yourself. Looking into the eyes of my baby daughter was a harrowing experience for me. She was helpless and fighting for her life, and my husband and I were responsible for keeping her alive. In spite of her frailty, we had to keep her strong. There was little I could do to stop the medical procedures that were being performed on her. Her life was full of pain.

Lester and I were children of the 1970s, pioneers living in the verdant woods of Oregon, forty miles from the nearest hospital. I was a registered nurse working in that hospital, financially supporting our plans for a life close to the earth, as Lester built our house. Torrential rains poured down on our partially constructed home during that bleak December. We lived in a trailer attached to the unfinished house, along a creek that had raged into a swollen river of logs and muck. It was a scene out of my favorite book, Ken Kesey's *Sometimes a Great Notion*. The sounds of a turbulent river haunt me to this day.

The rains didn't stop for weeks, forcing us to endure unrelenting cold, mud, sadness and fear those first weeks after our daughter's birth. I was as close to crazy as I've ever been in my life. Madness was a hair's breadth away. I have never felt so emotionally fragile.

Driving over an hour to the city of Medford for the daily hospital visit to our newborn, we looked like bedraggled, scruffy cats trudging into the sterile, antiseptic hallways of the pediatric ward. I hated my life during those days. The long drives to the hospital and the daily consultations with the doctor are moments that still reside in the pit of my stomach all these years later.

December is a hard-core month for me. Every year I feel the fragility of life at a cellular level.

I remember swaying back and forth in an old rocking chair that December, clutching a pillow instead of my newborn, totally unprepared for this catastrophe. My husband was also a wreck, trying to contain his own emotions as he drove us to and from the hospital through the unending rains. We lived for the moments each day when our doctor would tell us how much our baby weighed. Every ounce of weight gain was a cause for celebration.

The hospital Muzak played "I'll Be Home for Christmas" endlessly, and I asked the charge nurse to turn off the damnable song. But she couldn't honor my request because it was a recording loop from a central office in some faraway city. I never wept so much as I did during those first months of my daughter's life, and that song still sweeps me into a dark hole. In fact, most Christmas carols can put me over the edge, yet I listen to them nonstop. It's a weird dance of emotional extremes. *Feliz Navidad,* indeed.

For hours I sat in the neonatal intensive care unit, staring at the tiny pulsations of carotid blood flow on my daughter's neck as she slept. I was afraid to leave the hospital at night, afraid the pulse would stop and no one would be there to save her. My husband brought his guitar to the bedside and sang some favorite John Denver tunes as she slept in her plastic box. We were afraid she would hate John Denver as she got older, with buried memories surfacing in snippets of melodies.

But she held onto my finger with her tiny hand and never let go. And she likes John Denver.

We all survived those first weeks and years. All three of us—Lester, our little baby girl, and I— toughened up. And eventually the midnight visits to the emergency room and the hours of watching our daughter breathe in and out in her crib came to an end.

She made it. We made it too. Now married, and with a daughter of her own, she has grown into a beautiful, healthy young woman. That December also gave Lester and me what were probably among the best years of our marriage. We were a team, and we kept our little girl alive.

I think most December babies are unusually resilient. Maybe it's the cold, the wind, the wet. It builds grit. December is a bitter pill in rural Oregon, and babies somehow sweeten the acerbic taste of things. It is my Christmas reverie all these years later. Every December.

So what do these memories have to do with anything, really? What is it about Christmas and babies and death and vulnerability that put me in such a crazy place? I yo-yo back and forth, up and down, from feeling the sublime sacredness of the season to just closing my eyes and wishing for January and the new year.

MY FEET START to freeze up standing on the front door patio on this December morning in 2013. I love the long hours of darkness that come this time of year. Like a bear, I burrow into my own personal cave and hunker down in the darkness of the long nights, more contemplative. Idly, I wish the grandchildren would come for Christmas this year. But the kids and the grandkids are ensconced in their own traditions, their own trees and lights. If anything, we should go to them.

I take in the smells of this winter morning. The dogs' fur smells like wet chicken feathers. There's mesquite smoke and the faint perfume of desert creosote, which means there's rain in the air. I sprinkle fish food into the icy goldfish pond and watch it skitter across the frozen surface. Taking a nearby shovel, I poke at the frigid water, and the fish sluggishly rise and look at me with their fish eyes. Spidery tendrils of cracks spread on the ice like fast-growing tree roots. The tendrils act as if they're alive, spreading their lacy pattern across the pond. The broken ice squeaks and groans. The fish pop up to the surface, and do their morning dance, mouths wide open. Breakfast!

Crimson clouds appear in the east. The sun is taking its sweet time at the break of day. I sniff the air and smell rain, maybe snow. Finally, the sun pierces through a few layers of gun-metal gray stratus clouds edged in brilliant splashes of gold.

I grin and watch the rising sun.

LAST NIGHT WE hosted a holiday open house, and the remnants of wine and rich foods are still sitting in my gut like a dead weight. For the first time in three decades, I have a hangover. Taking several deep breaths, I do my best to clear my head and take in the crystalline stillness of this desert scene.

The birds that have decided to spend the winter here are picking at the icy water in the bird-bath. Crazy birds. Go south, you goldfinches, go south to Mexico and find yourself a condo and some indulgent Americans with sacks of birdseed. The goldfinches skate across the frozen birdbath like little drunken ballerinas.

Gazing across the canyon, I imagine the iconic image of the season—a pregnant Mary with her husband, Joseph, leading a donkey as they trek through the desert looking for shelter. Absently I wonder if there is anyone out there now. Perhaps some migrants are heading north from Mexico, dodging the authorities, walking toward Tucson.

Maybe a jaguar or a Mexican wolf is scaring up some morning fare. Peering into the distance, I see nothing moving. The desert is a frozen stillness. The idea of spending the night in frigid temperatures is more than my head can handle. It's time go inside the house and swallow a couple of aspirin.

Tamale, the feral cat that hangs out on the roof, is staring at me, wondering when the food bowl gets replenished. She may be feral and hunt down fresh meat each day, but the creature comforts of some ready-made cat food are never disdained. Tamale's bed is a scruffy piece of fake lamb's wool draped on the patio stairs, and on this morning it's stiff with frost. I privately worry about Tamale on these freezing December nights. It's almost Christmas. Why won't she come in and settle by the fire at night? Piling an old fluffy robe on a patio chair, I hope Tamale will snuggle into the fleece when the winter winds drop the temperatures well below freezing. She's adamant about spending her time outside. Coming inside is for pussies. Tamale is a tiger cat.

The house is a shambles. Paper plates, leftover food, and partially filled glasses of wine litter the living room. My slippers stick to the floor where puddles of tequila and champagne spot the Mexican tiles. I can smell the acrid sweetness of spilled alcohol, and a surging throb of pain passes behind my reddened eyes. This is going to be one dismal day of hard labor. I don't care if I ever see another tortilla chip or bowl of guacamole again. It's time to retrieve the mop and bucket and get cracking on a thorough clean-up.

But first, some more strong coffee and a couple of aspirin.

"How about a fire this morning?" I say to Lester. "It looks like we're socked in all day with these clouds. Whatever happened to the Arizona sun?" My voice is a croaky whine.

Looking out at the drizzle and the blue fog capping the mountains, I idly think about who might be out there. Are the migrants from Mexico trying to cross today? How could they possibly survive in this cold and wet? Quickly I dismiss the whole idea. It's just too uncomfortable to consider.

We live close to the Mexican border, and the struggles of the migrants are close to our home. A drive to the grocery store is a half-hour trip, during which I often see a lineup of young men sitting on the shoulder of a country road, Border Patrol agents pacing back and forth before them. The whole scene casts a pall on the wild beauty of the desert. Good will toward men, indeed.

Once a week I drive to Nogales, Mexico, with the Green Valley/ Sahuarita Samaritans, a group of humanitarian aid workers. We serve breakfast to a roomful of pilgrims heading north, heading south, and heading any direction they can to survive. I hand out clothes and lend an ear to the stories and tragedies of a national policy that criminalizes the migration of desperate people.

But on this December day, you'd have to be out of your mind to be trekking across the desert.

Peering into the refrigerator, I grab a green corn tamale, some *frijoles*, and *queso fresco* (a crumbly Mexican cheese) left from the holiday feast. Together with some strong coffee and the aspirin, I dig into a delicious morning-after breakfast. We'll be picking at party remnants for days. A half-full bottle of champagne sits on the kitchen counter, losing all its fizz. The dogs are licking the floor clean of tortilla crumbs and cookies. Candle wax has melted over my special candle holders and onto my favorite holiday tablecloth.

With the miracle of caffeine buzzing through my cerebral cortex, I pour water into a bucket and grab the mop. First I'll tackle the tile floors and then graduate toward the disasters and spills on the furniture. It all feels like penance after a night of pleasant debauchery. I'm paying the piper.

———————— • ————————

HOURS PASS. IT'S three o'clock in the afternoon, and the house-cleaning chores are getting done. I'm drinking a lot of coffee and listening to Linda Ronstadt singing carols. In quiet exasperation, I mop up the sticky floor, muttering that this is the last holiday party I will host. The last.

The dogs are raising holy hell about something outside in the winter drizzle. Probably a band of *javelinas,* the wild pig-like hoofed mammals that roam the Arizona desert. Maybe a hawk closing in on one of the bird feeders. Maybe nothing. The dogs love to bark at absolutely nothing. My mood is foul.

The barking persists and I do my best to ignore the racket. They're just being dogs, and that's what dogs do. They bark at stuff.

Glancing out the window, leaning on my mop, I see both dogs staring toward the far side of the canyon gorge, barking like they mean business. The drizzle is lightening and the sun beginning to poke through. In fact there's a rainbow toward the Santa Rita Mountains. Sun shining on our snowy gorge creates clouds of steam and vapor. I think of the musical, "Brigadoon," about the mythical village rising from the mist. A moment of magic.

Food, coffee, the mindless task of cleaning the house, and the sun sparkling on the new-fallen snow make for a satisfying day. I look forward to a quiet evening with friends at a nearby ranch. It will be good to relax and connect with the neighbors during this special season. Peace on Earth has come to our little valley. Saying a silent prayer of thanksgiving for my health, a good husband, and the quiet life we have in these mountains, I sing along with the Christmas carols on the CD player.

But the dogs keep barking. I step out into the icy drizzle with a mop in my hand.

Initially dazzled by the glare of the sun on the snow, I see a figure lurching toward the edge of the canyon. With a garbage bag flapping wildly around his frame, a man's words travel distinctly across the steep canyon: "Help me, help me. I am lost. My heart … it is dying."

He holds one hand to his chest and leans into a walking stick. He teeters. He staggers to the edge of the gorge that separates us, a serious drop of eighty or more feet. Our house, sitting on the edge of a canyon, commands a view of the river running through it. Crossing from one side to the other takes skill, or the agility of the *javelinas* that scale the canyon walls with no problem at all. It is a steep, treacherous, rocky cliff.

"How do I get across?" he asks, half in Spanish. Pointing west, I tell him that there is an easier crossing about a half mile down the canyon. He waves and begins walking.

Lester joins me outside and we look at each other.

"I think he's a migrant and he's lost," I tell him.

"Well, let's see if he makes it over to this side. He may just keep going and follow the canyon to the freeway."

"But that's at least fifteen miles. I don't think he can make it before dark."

Back inside, I stoke the fire and put on some fresh coffee. The place still looks like hell in spite of my housecleaning efforts, and now we may have an unexpected guest. Dashing around the room, I gather up some remaining plastic cups of wine, paper plates of cookies, and dried-up guacamole. It's close to four o'clock, and the sun is rapidly descending. I'm feeling a combination of dread, panic, and curiosity about the man covered in the black trash bag.

Because our house is built in a rugged area of rocks, canyons, cacti and periodically a river of monsoon rains or melted snow, rarely do migrants pass through here. It's simply too difficult to hike through the trackless terrain. Travelers from Mexico and Central America choose more accessible trails. Privately I'm relieved about this. The realities of responding to lost, desperate people on our land stretch my humanitarian ideals. On the one hand, I want to help people reach their destination and keep them safe. On the other, I want a life that's not in perpetual rescue mode.

But here we are. There's a man out there wearing a black trash bag, and he looks like he needs help.

We have plans for tonight, a special holiday dinner at a neighbor's house. And then in two days is the biggest party of the year at a nearby ranch. I don't have time to deal with this. I'm ashamed to admit that I hope this fellow in the black trash bag will keep on moving. It's Christmas. I've got enough on my mind without an interloper disrupting my plans.

The dogs begin carrying on again. Looking out the window, I now see a figure shrouded in a wet bag standing on our patio. Like a wounded black raven, he half collapses beside the patio table. When I open the door, we lock eyes. His are reddened and full of tears; mine are wide and wary. He looks to be in desperate shape. I immediately drop my defenses, step outside and take his arm, supporting him as he stumbles to the door.

"Please help me," he chokes out. He drops his backpack and a plastic water bottle half full of an amber liquid falls out. It looks like apple juice. Maybe it is apple juice. Or maybe it's urine. Drinking urine is the last resort when thirst is your constant companion. As our December pilgrim lifts the trash bag over his head, I pick up the plastic bottle, remove the lid, and sniff. The distinct odor of concentrated urine fills my nostrils. I attempt to do this surreptitiously while he is peeling off his trash bag, trying to pretend I don't know what's in the bottle. But when I face our disheveled guest, our eyes meet again. He sees me sniffing the bottle. He looks embarrassed, and quickly averts his gaze, looking down. I feel like I've trespassed into his private soul and quickly put down the water bottle. He turns his back to me, petting the dogs, who are ecstatic. Tails wagging furiously, both dogs give welcoming licks to this sojourner from the desert. They inhale our guest, licking and nudging and loving the smells of dirt and dung and urine.

I pay attention to the dogs, who are shrewd judges of character. They look like they're greeting a long-lost friend. Arroya, who's deaf, is licking the stranger's sodden shoes. (We surmise that as a tiny puppy, Arroya probably landed on her head when she was tossed into a desert canyon in mid-January, left to freeze.) Meanwhile, Cassie herds our guest, pushing his legs toward the door.

I open the door wider and help him inside, where he strips off his tattered jacket and looks around the living room. He's shivering, and his face is flushed and hot. His gait is unsteady as he walks to the fireplace and holds his hands to the flames to warm them. Caked with dirt, he rubs his numb fingers. His clothes are wet and dank, and his jeans are ripped. I can smell him from ten feet away: an acrid odor of damp earth, the stench of an unwashed body, and urine.

He straightens his body, standing taller, lifting his chin, and introduces himself with great dignity. "My name is Juan Carlos. I am lost. I am from Guatemala." His English is reasonably good. Sprinkling his words with Spanish, he is easily understood by both my husband and me.

"My name is Peg. My given name in Spanish would be Margarita. This is *mi esposo*, Lester."

Steadying himself, he leans against the couch. The skin on his face is an ashen gray; his hands are bright red, and the tips of his fingers are pallid and white. He rubs his hands together some more, then pauses and buries them in Arroya's furry coat. His body is trembling.

"May I have some water, *por favor*?"

I snap to it.

"Oh my God, of course, of course. Would you like some coffee? Would you like some food?"

I leap into action and fetch this man some needed liquids. I am a retired nurse, and yet my training feels a thousand miles away. But my brain comes to life, and I spring into nurse mode. Water. Coffee. Tortillas. Chips. Dips. Tamales. We have it all. We have party food. This man is starving.

Pulling things out of the refrigerator, I prepare a tray of tortilla chips, salsa, and a tamale—leftovers from our holiday soirée. Even a couple of cookies. I place a hot cup of black coffee and a glass of water before our exhausted guest. Sitting on the couch, he devours everything on the tray and asks for more coffee. I leap into action again, pouring more coffee and offering crackers, cheese, carrot sticks.

After about twenty minutes, he asks where the bathroom is located. Soon I can hear retching and vomiting.

Chiding myself, I realize that serving a feast to a starving man is not prudent.

What are you thinking? Put away the tamales. Stop bringing out the chips and dips. Slow down. Get a grip. Start with a simple diet of clear liquids.

This man is in critical condition. He can't handle the richness of my offering. The fragility of this human life becomes apparent. The man is in trouble. Maybe I should take him to the local hospital. What if he dies here? What am I really trying to accomplish? What should we do? *Proceed with caution. Use your head.*

Who is this stranger?

Rifling through a drawer, I find my stethoscope and blood pressure cuff. *Breathe deeply*, I tell myself. *Get yourself grounded and remember the basic rules of emergency nursing care. Get this man's vital signs. Take his pulse, respirations, temperature, and blood pressure. Collect the data. Come up with a plan.*

When Juan Carlos comes back from the bathroom, he's pasty white and shaky. Looking embarrassed, he sniffs the armpits of his tattered blue-plaid flannel shirt and motions to me to keep a distance. "I smell bad, like a pig," he says, shaking his head, grimacing and looking shame-faced.

I sit him on the couch and take his vital signs. I touch him in spite of his admonitions about his filth, his smell. Pulse is thready and rapid. Temperature is 100 degrees. Blood pressure is elevated. His skin is hot to the touch, and he's alternately shivering and sweating. I see beads of perspiration on his forehead.

Looking at Lester, who's hovering at the side of the room keeping his distance, I suggest that he take Juan Carlos into the guest room and show him the shower. I'll rummage through the closet and find some clean clothes, a pair of socks, and maybe some tennis shoes that will fit. The man seems frightened, cautious and spacey. We're all circling each other like vigilant desert creatures, sniffing out the situation.

I feel like I'm operating in a dream, with my feet not quite touching the ground.

Explaining in my broken Spanish that the winter drizzle will turn to a snowfall tonight, I invite Juan Carlos to stay in our home until he's stronger and can continue his journey. Lester nods his approval. Juan Carlos's face shows relief and he nods his head with a wan smile.

I realize I don't know what his journey is.

"So, where are you going? Do you have family in *los Estados Unidos?*"

"*Mi hermana* (my sister) is in Nashville," he responds. "I am going to Nashville, where I have a job promised to me. I will send money home to my family in Guatemala. I can work in a Japanese restaurant. I make sushi." His mood sounds upbeat as he explains his plan.

So Juan Carlos is a sushi chef. This man who has entered our life looking like Moses coming across the desert with his staff and a shiny black plastic robe flapping in the wind is a man from Guatemala, with a sister in Nashville, Tennessee. He's skilled in the art of Japanese sushi-making, and he sits in our living room in the middle of the Sonoran Desert with fierce determination in his eyes. Now this is true globalization.

Short in stature, Juan Carlos has closely cropped black hair framing his round face. He looks like an indigenous person, possibly Mayan or *mixta* (mixed race). He wears a ripped nylon down jacket that is dirt-brown, festooned with a mesquite branch poking out of one seam. Bloody scratches zig-zag across his wrists. The creases of his hands and nails are blackened with dried blood and red desert clay, and healing bruises spot his forearms in shades of yellow and green. His tennis shoes are coming apart at the seams and are caked with the grime of many miles. Bare toes poke through his tattered socks and out the seams of his shoes.

He looks around the room at the candles burning and the Christmas crèche displayed on the mantle. "Is this a church?"

I smile. "No, this is definitely not a church."

The house does look like a holy temple of some sort. It's Christmas, and I've pulled out all the stops. Candles flicker, Nat King Cole is singing about chestnuts roasting on an open fire, and images of the *Virgen de Guadalupe* are everywhere. I'm beating back the demons.

"You are an angel, and God has put you in my path," he tells me.

I blink awkwardly. We both sit on the couch. I can't hold his gaze and quickly look away. No one has ever called me an angel before. Not like this, anyway. I feel a blush creep up my neck and face and simply sit there.

I change the subject.

"Would you like to take a shower now?"

Lester shows our unexpected guest into the bedroom, and I follow with an armload of clean clothes. Explaining the idiosyncrasies of the hot and cold shower faucet, Juan Carlos nods in appreciation, looks at us and whispers many times, "*Gracias.*"

Once he's out of sight, I cautiously relax. I still have my doubts about this guy. I wonder if I should hide anything. The car keys? The checkbook? Credit cards? Should I just take this stranger to a hospital?

And then there are the guns. Lester is a gun guy and has stashed guns behind doors and in closets for his target practice or to scare off the coyotes when they get too close to the dogs. The guns are loaded, always.

I've known Juan Carlos for thirty minutes, and here we are escorting him into the guest bedroom with clean clothes, towels, more water, and trust.

The thought of calling the Border Patrol or law enforcement never enters my mind. Or Lester's.

However, the image of a Border Patrol agent aggressively knocking on our door does enter my mind. I'm afraid of getting caught with an undocumented person in the back bedroom. No doubt about that.

We will help this person, and just follow our gut instincts. We will trust that he's who he says he is: a lost young man in the middle of the desert on the darkest night of the year. It is the winter solstice, and this is no night to close our door to a stranger. At this point I trust Juan Carlos more than I trust the Border Patrol. We will improvise.

And yet he is still a stranger. The other. An outsider.

And I'm worried. About the law, about others who may be hiding outside waiting for nightfall, ready to break into our peaceful life, about what we're going to do with this beaten-down soul. I was brought up to avoid people who are different. Those early lessons stay buried in a deep dark place, and they're rearing their ugliness at this moment.

TWO

Chicago Roots

Margarita

I GREW UP on the South Side of Chicago, and for the first twelve years of my life, my parents warned against the encroaching waves of black people that would disrupt our Irish-Catholic white middle-class neighborhood. My father bragged that any black face that showed up in our lily-white enclave would disappear. During the late 1940s and 1950s, Chicago was among the most segregated cities in the country. There were regions of different ethnic neighborhoods—the Polish, the Italians, the Greeks, the African-Americans, the Chinese, and my own Irish-Catholic environs. People of color rarely ventured outside the boundaries of their neighborhoods.

"Any nigger that comes within a mile is a dead man," my father would invoke, downing a Blatz beer and scattering cigarette ashes at the kitchen table, where he held forth on Chicago politics. I took his words literally. My Dad was an attorney in the Loop in downtown Chicago. His opinions about race, color and ethnicity were entrenched in white-supremacy vitriol. My imagination went wild with visions of violence and mayhem. I think my Dad figured that this would make me feel safe. It was a white-bread community; there were no brown or black faces.

I was taught to fear people who didn't look like me, eat like me, or talk like me. I was told not to sit next to people of color on the bus because they smell bad. They certainly didn't go to my all-white school.

"They stick to their own kind," was a frequently heard response in our South-Side Chicago neighborhood. Riding the "el" downtown with me, my Dad would point out the trash and the decrepit condition of the slums as we sped by the backyards of the growing African-American neighborhoods. Many were fleeing the southern states for the jobs and the promise of the cities up north. My parents were terrified of this migration, and I was taught what streets were the boundaries of our community.

"Never cross beyond Seventy-second and Loomis. It's dangerous. Be polite, but never talk to one of them. They aren't like us. Stick to your own kind." I wasn't exactly taught to hate, but I definitely was taught to fear. And I was told that white people were better than people of color. Many times.

In my Chicago neighborhood, white home-owners banded together and signed agreements in which they stipulated that if they ever moved, they would never sell their homes to black families. My father signed one of those agreements. Occasionally, a white home-owner would refuse to go along with the agreement, and a black family would "invade" an all-white neighborhood. When the rare black family moved into my neighborhood, people were often harassed and sometimes violently attacked. People of color were ostracized and frequently moved back to less desirable neighborhoods even though they were financially able to live where there were better schools and housing.

I have no memory of talking to an African-American person during the first twelve years of my life. There were no people of color at my elementary school. I heard every epithet directed toward African-Americans, Mexicans, Italians, Polish, Chinese, and Jews in my childhood home. In the museums and public buildings of 1940s Chicago, I saw signs on bathroom doors and water fountains for "colored" and "white only." I ate in restaurants and stayed in hotels where people of color weren't allowed. I thought this was normal.

My elementary school was a microcosm of my neighborhood. I remember one little boy of Greek descent. My parents told me he was "just off the boat." His family owned a Greek restaurant. I don't recall anyone ever speaking to this child, who had dark skin, was very shy and small in stature, and struggled with his school-work as he was learning to speak English. He looked like he needed a bath and wore the same clothes day after day. I never forgot this child and can still picture his small slumped-over body sitting in the back of the classroom, never saying a word. Reaching out to this child did not occur to me, and yet I remember him clearly sixty years later, sitting in the last row in a faded, tattered flannel shirt and pants that were hiked up with a thin rope for a belt.

In the summer of 1955, when I was twelve, Emmett Till, an African-American Chicago boy of fourteen, was brutally murdered and mutilated while visiting relatives in Mississippi during the summer. I remember my parents talking about this horrific killing around the dinner table. The young teenage boy had entered a small grocery store in a tiny Mississippi town and flirted openly with the white woman behind the counter, allegedly asking her for a date. The woman claimed he "forced himself" on her, grabbing her, trying to hug her. Four days later, Emmett Till was thrown into the Tallahatchie River, tied to a cotton gin fan with barbed wire. His eye was gouged out and he'd been shot in the head by the woman's husband and other family members. Emmett Till's tragic death was one of the sparks that ignited the African-American civil rights movement in this country.

In 2007 this same woman admitted that she had made up the most damning part of the story and that young Emmett Till had not assaulted her. *The Blood of Emmett Till*, by Timothy Tyson, published in 2017, revealed the lies and secrets that the young woman from behind the counter had kept for over fifty years.

Emmett's murder made a strong impression on me. Struggling to figure out what behaviors were appropriate and correct and what actions could get you killed, I was afraid to look at black people on the buses and the "el" train. Talking to anyone with dark skin was *verboten*. They were the "other," and they had their own culture, language, and ways of living. Our family lived a life in Chicago that was insulated and racist.

One of my struggles as a child was reconciling this fact: My direct heritage was German, and the United States had been at war with Germany and Hitler. So why was it okay to be of German descent but not okay to be an African-American? We weren't at war with Africa. We had just defeated the Nazis and Hitler, and the images of the Holocaust were now on the evening news. In my own developing mind, it seemed to me that the Germans were more of a threat in our neighborhood than any person with dark skin.

My family left our Chicago neighborhood in 1957 and moved to Tucson. Our lives changed dramatically. While looking for a house to rent that first year, my parents had some trepidation about living in a neighborhood with Mexicans and African-Americans. The city was much more integrated than Chicago.

For a year we rented a house and lived next to a Mexican-American family. There was frequent noise and laughter and gifts of tamales passed over the patio wall. Dad loved the tequila that our new neighbors generously shared. In Tucson, people with dark skin weren't treated like they were invisible or inferior. In fact, they were the politicos and business people who ran the city. And they seemed to be having a lot of fun. The children next door ran wild in the streets, kicking a soccer ball with their bare feet. My brothers and I watched with envy. We were no longer big city Chicago kids; now we were finding our way in the desert sun and streets of Tucson.

But the deeply ingrained sense of *diferente* was embedded in my psyche. As much as I wanted to belong and to connect with my new Latino and African-American friends in Tucson, I couldn't. Always there was a wall, a barrier, a speck of fear. I couldn't invite them into my childhood home. Fearing that my father would call them a racial epithet, I was careful about who came by for a visit. I couldn't get Emmett Till out of my mind. Maybe someone would get killed if I messed with the complicated and confusing code of conduct that permeated white culture.

When I played in my high school band, however, I began to enjoy fun times with Latinos and African-American band members. During school dances, I learned all the newest steps and rhythms from people of color. Never discussing this with my parents, I had a secret life. The civil rights marches during the 1960s in the South both frightened and fascinated me. I wanted to participate but didn't know how.

Fast-forward to me standing in my home on this dark December night fifty-five years later. I'm contemplating how far I have left to go. The old kernel of fear sits like an irritating piece of popcorn in the back of my throat. It isn't choking me, but sticks in my craw. Looking at Juan Carlos as he stumbles into the back bedroom, I wonder what in the hell Lester and I are getting ourselves into. I am inviting Juan Carlos into our home, but he is the "other," and I'm not sure where all of this is going.

Running scared, I carefully hide my turquoise Indian jewelry in the back of a dresser drawer. Outside, I take the car keys out of the front seat console and put them in my purse. Then I hide my purse.

I am ten years old again, back in Chicago, worried about the "other."

THREE

⟹ • ⟸

Chiquita Banana

THERE ARE COMPELLING reasons why Juan Carlos has landed on our doorstep, more dead than alive. His reasons for risking his life in the desert are connected to poverty, a lack of work, political corruption and gang violence. This is not a coming-of-age odyssey where young men travel to *el norte* seeking their fortune and hoping for a life of prosperity in *los Estados Unidos*. This is a journey of survival. For Juan Carlos, there are no other options.

In the summer of 2014, many people from Guatemala, El Salvador, and Honduras are fleeing to the north. Young children have traveled thousands of miles, often hand in hand with a teenage sister or brother, and have crossed our borders asking for help. Their choices are few: either stay at home and starve or be killed. Or migrate.

How did we get to this point? What would move a parent in Guatemala to send a seven-year-old child on a journey of over a thousand miles without adult supervision? Why are so many people in Central America on the move?

The reasons for the civil disruption in Central America are intrinsically entangled with policies of the United States that have gone horribly awry. For over one hundred years, the United States' relations with Latin America have received low priority, no matter who is president or which party is in power. We don't pay attention to what is going on there.

And then when catastrophe hits, we ask, "Why are these people trying to enter our country? Why can't they fix whatever is wrong in their own country?"

Our record of unilateral force is long and troubling. When something happens in Latin America that upsets Washington and violates our sense of order in the Western Hemisphere—or, more precisely, menaces American interests—we respond with force. We reach for our guns. And rarely does anyone question our actions and motives.

For a century we referred to the nations of Central America as "banana republics," functioning at the beck and call of the United Fruit Company. In 1901 the United Fruit Company, a U.S. company based in Boston, had begun a long and complicated relationship with Guatemala. The company introduced the United States and the world to bananas, and soon it dominated almost a dozen countries in Latin America.

During the 1950s, United Fruit created a cartoon character named Chiquita Banana, and this dancing figure with the headdress of fruit piled high is still a popular figure for anyone living in the twentieth century. Every child born in the 1940s can sing the first few lines of this song:

> "I'm Chiquita Banana and I've come to say,
> Bananas have to ripen in a certain way.
> When they are fleck'd with brown and have a golden hue,
> Bananas taste the best and are the best for you."

The people of North America had to learn how to eat and store bananas, and the Chiquita Banana song tutored housewives about this exotic new fruit. Today the banana is the world's fourth major food, after rice, wheat and milk. Before 1901 and the cultivation and sale of bananas, this fruit was virtually unknown in most of the world. The United Fruit Company owned the market for a hundred years.

Guatemala was chosen as the original site by the United Fruit Company in the early 1900s because at the time, that country's government was weak, corrupt, and easily manipulated. The company bought up land in Guatemala in order to squeeze out any competition and simply let the land lie fallow.

During the 1950s, a left-leaning democratically elected president, Jacobo Árbenz, decided to redistribute the fallow land to the peasants and farmers, continuing a program of reforms that had been initiated by his predecessor in that office, Juan José Arévalo. The Árbenz government bought the property from the United Fruit Company at the market price, and the U.S. government wasn't happy with this transaction. America's fear at that time was communism, and under pressure from United Fruit, the Eisenhower administration made it a mission of the Central Intelligence Agency to keep Latin America "safe for democracy."

Árbenz was ousted in a 1954 coup engineered by the U.S. Department of State and the Central Intelligence Agency. The country's new president, Carlos Castillo Armas, reversed the land reforms of Árbenz, and what followed was four decades of bloody revolution (Armas himself being assassinated in 1957), ending what had been a hopeful decade of reform and prosperity.

From 1960 to 1996, a bewildering succession of rulers and governments prevailed, most of them military. The majority of the victims of the continuous forty-year civil war were indigenous peoples of leftist persuasion. Warfare between peasant guerrilla groups and the government continued, leaving two hundred thousand dead in Guatemala, and tens of thousands throughout Latin America. The United States entrusted its interest to petty dictators and military generals who enriched themselves at our expense. Democracy faded, and authoritarian rule dominated the landscape.

And here is the sad truth: Over those four decades, the Guatemalan government murdered huge numbers of its own citizens in order to survive. Human rights advocates from the United States and elsewhere were labeled communist sympathizers because they supported the guerrilla forces opposing the oppressive government officials. Many church missions and nongovernmental organizations were targeted, and members were tortured and assassinated.

In 1996 the United Nations facilitated a peace negotiation acknowledging the rights of the indigenous Indian population, and Guatemala's decades of civil war came to an end. The peace has been fragile and there is lingering volatility, but there have been a number of democratic elections. Citizens have pushed for a stronger rule of law, and the people have demanded accountability within the judicial system.

And then there's the drug trade, with Guatemala acting as a geographical corridor between Honduras and the United States. Land-based shipments of cocaine dramatically increased from 2008 to 2016. Mexican drug cartels are present in Guatemala, ensuring the successful passage of illicit drugs into the lucrative markets of U.S. cities. Drug money is a key source in financing political parties in Guatemala, and children are often forced to join gangs and participate in the drug trade. It's business.

The insatiable drug appetites of Americans fuel the black market of drugs grown and processed south of the border. No one really knows how many billions of dollars are exchanged between the United States and Latin America, but drugs are a major component of the economies of Central America and Mexico.

Villages and cities in Guatemala are overrun with gangs that traffic illicit drugs to the United States. Young people are recruited to help transport the lucrative product north. When an indigenous family is struggling and there isn't enough food on the table, carrying a load of marijuana or cocaine seems a logical option. Legitimate work that pays a fair wage is impossible to find. The dangers of drug trafficking seem to be a reasonable chance to take, despite the possibility of death and torture. Many have no choice.

Out of this political chaos, many young men and women flee to the United States. Parents decide that the perilous journey to the north is the best chance for their children's survival. And many of these refugees—children and adults alike—are apprehended at our borders.

In the summer of 2014 (six months after my encounter with Juan Carlos), a warehouse in Nogales, Arizona, housed more than twenty-four hundred children under the age of eighteen. Homeland Security and Border Patrol agents did their best to care for these children, who were confused, traumatized, and desperate. Most were seeking to join parents and relatives who already lived in the United States. The children were being housed, fed, and had access to hot showers and toilets. They marched like little soldiers back and forth, from one building to the next, their hands clasped behind their backs. I watched them through a cyclone fence, and was not allowed into the sleeping quarters to visit with the detained children. It was a sobering, troubling sight. They naturally missed their parents, and the warehouse was a silent witness to their tears every night.

I spoke with one of the Homeland Security agents during this time of crisis. She told me she would go home late at night after spending eight hours with the children and would be unable to sleep. So she would return at 3 a.m. to the warehouse to help settle the children. She would read stories to the young ones and rock them to sleep. The large room with hundreds of floor mats would be filled with the muffled sobs of children, terrified, lost, and wondering what would happen to them. The sound of crinkling, metallic all-weather blankets could be heard as the children tossed and turned during their restless nights.

A Tucson attorney who was on an official visit to the warehouse told me she had encountered one little girl sitting in a corner, rocking back and forth on the floor, wringing her hands, saying, "How will my mother ever find me here? Look at all of these children! How will she ever know where I am?"

"I will never forget you," the attorney told her. "I will do everything I can to find your mother."

I think about this little girl often and hope this attorney or some kindly bureaucratic official helped this child locate her mother.

FOUR

═══ • ═══

The Journey

TODAY, ON DECEMBER 21, 2013, I contemplate Juan Carlos's journey and the turbulence of his home country. This is not his first trek to *el norte*. He has walked the migrant trail before, making it to Nashville, but when his mother became ill in 2009, he returned to his home village in Guatemala.

He tells me some of his history.

Juan Carlos was born in 1986 in a small agrarian community near the west coast of Guatemala. His village was poor and work was scarce. There was drug trafficking through his village, and children were recruited to help in the transport of cocaine and heroin that came up from Honduras and Colombia. Juan Carlos had family contacts in Nashville, so in 2007 he decided that because times were desperate, he needed to make a bold move. He migrated to Nashville and found work at a Japanese restaurant.

After a few years, he returned to Guatemala to help care for his mother, who was suffering from severe headaches and had taken to her bed. He met his wife, Maria, and they had two children. In 2011, however, Juan Carlos once again journeyed to the United States, crossing at the Texas border. He was caught in Texas and spent some time in a detention center in McAllen before being deported back to Guatemala.

Now, in 2013, he decided to return to Nashville where he had the promise of a job at the same Japanese restaurant. He would send money back to his wife in Guatemala. Maybe the laws in the United States would change, making it easier for families to be together. He would work hard. He would learn English. He would prosper. It was a simple straightforward plan.

The overriding issue was this: Chances were high that U.S. Border Patrol agents would catch him, or he would die en route.

———⟹ • ⟸———

December 17, 2013
Juan Carlos

THE ROAD SIGN says Patagonia. *Jesucristo.* I thought Patagonia was someplace in South America. But we must be in Arizona. The signs are in English, and the cars are all Hondas. We've been walking four days, and the *pollero* (slang for guide) keeps yelling, "Faster, faster!" He kicked one of the women in the stomach this morning because she didn't get up fast enough, and she rolled on the earth in pain, moaning and clutching her waist. I glanced at some of the other men and felt shame and disgust with myself. What kind of a man allows a woman to be kicked like a dog?

We are the *pollos* (chickens), and the guide is our *pollero.* I think about the many times I have kicked a chicken. And a dog, too. At this moment we are lower than the beasts.

There are two *polleros.* One is a leader, while the other walks in the rear of our bedraggled group. We are pilgrims on a mission. We are looking for the promised land.

One of the *polleros* tells us Tucson is just over those mountains. Not too far. Just over there. "Keep going," he says. "Here. Take these pills for energy." I swallow two pills and wait for the buzz to kick in.

We will stop to rest in this *arroyo* for a few hours. It's cold, but he tells us we can't build a fire. There are eighteen of us. Ten are women. How they manage, I don't know. The women hold each other for warmth. Three men are carrying marijuana, the drug none of us can afford. Only the *americanos*.

I have made a pact with one of the travelers. We will stick together, protect the women if we can, and help each other if we stumble. He is from Honduras, and his life sounds worse than mine, if that is possible. We both talk about our families, our wives, our children. He is two years older than me, and this is his third try to cross into *los Estados Unidos*. His brother lives in South Carolina.

"Is that closer than Nashville? Maybe there is work for me in South Carolina?"

"Maybe," my Honduran friend answers as he fumbles with a match, trying to light a cigarette.

I have never been so cold. I thought we would be walking in a desert. This is no desert. There is nothing here but rocks and thorns and cold that licks at my bones. I can no longer feel my feet. Looking down at my shoes I see that the toes on my left foot are peeking through the mesh of the tennis shoes I was given at a place they call *el comedor* in Nogales. I found a jacket there as well, and the food that was served gave me strength for this leg of my journey.

There were prayers for my safety. The Catholic sisters at *el comedor* told the men who were crossing to stay together and protect the women. I hang my head; I am a miserable failure.

Taking a seat on a jagged rock that is wet, the icy water soaking through my jeans to my already freezing butt, I pull out some tortillas that taste like cardboard. Not like the ones from home, thick and warm from the oven. The Mexicans don't know how to make a decent tortilla. They are made of flour, not corn. It is like eating burnt paper. Tasteless. But I wolf it down. My candy bars I'll save for later, my reward when I reach my ride in Tucson. Only a little farther, our *coyote* (another slang word for "guide") tells us. I peer into the distance, looking for the lights of Tucson, but see nothing.

Darkness comes fast, and with it the cold. Last night was the worst. I could not stop shaking. I dream of Maria and the *hijos* (children), Juanito and Lupita. I dream of tortillas that smell of the corn *masa* of my home town. Not these crappy, thin flour pieces of shit that have no nourishment.

Mi amigo Humberto has a small camper's stove, and we slip away from the group to light it and warm our hands. I close my eyes and imagine the coffee fields and sunshine of my home in the mountains of Guatemala. But mostly I dream of Maria and our warm bed, the children snuggled in with us each night. The small camp stove gives off a little warmth, and we hover around our tiny beacon of light and hope.

Suddenly the *pollero* appears, kicks the stove off its rocky perch, and pushes Humberto to the ground. Then a sharp pain in my groin stuns me as the boots of the *pollero* find their mark. Somersaulting into the thorns of the creosote bush, I roll into a ball to protect myself, rocking back and forth in agony. A flashlight shines in my face, blinding me to the assault. My hands shield my crotch and I brace myself for another kick.

"You want *la migra* (Border Patrol) to find us and haul us all off to jail?" he bellows.

"No fires, for Christ sake. You can be spotted a mile away. *La migra* is everywhere tonight, and you'll get us all killed!"

"We're just trying to keep warm," I tell the *pollero*. "I can't feel my hands or feet anymore." I am whimpering and frightened like a baby.

"Keep moving and you'll warm up."

It is starting to rain lightly, and it feels like there is ice mixed in with the rain. It all falls gently, like a slow-motion movie. This is going to be a long night. There is no way I can rest in this icy rain. Pulling a trash bag over my head I crouch under a rocky ledge and try to sleep. I can't stop shaking.

I think about Nashville, and my sister who waits for me. Drifting off, I try to rest in this soaking, rocky landscape. I hear my sister talking to me, and I smile as I shiver in this wet hell-hole. "There is a restaurant that wants to hire you," she says. "It is a Japanese restaurant, and you can make sushi and noodles again."

I quietly laugh out loud, remembering my time in Nashville in 2007 and the little printed kerchief I wore around my head. I learned to make fancy sushi dishes and put them on little boats that floated around the bar in the restaurant. There I was, a Guatemalan boy making fancy Japanese sushi for gringo cowboys in Nashville. For two years I created exotic sushi with raw, smelly fish and sticky rice. Slowly, I was turning into an *americano,* more or less. A Japanese *americano,* with a red kerchief tied around my head to disguise my Guatemalan face. Soon I will be back in Nashville and will send my earnings home to Maria.

When *mi madre* became sick several years ago, with headaches that kept her up all night thrashing in the bed, I had to go home to her. Truth be told, I missed my mother and my life in the highlands.

But when I returned to my village in 2009, it did not feel like the same place. There were gangs in the streets, and my mother's headaches tormented her all the more because she was terrified. My father was one of the teachers at the school. He was afraid of the *policia* and the military trucks in the streets, and often he was even afraid of his students. Many days he stayed home. How can you teach mathematics when the bullets zing through the windows and the children are lying on the floor to stay clear of the flying glass?

The marijuana was growing in the coffee fields, and the gangs bundled their green treasure. I almost hired on with one of the cartels. A hundred thousand *quetzales* to drive a load to Xela. More than I make in a year in the fields—if I get paid at all, that is.

I tried to return to Nashville in 2011 but was picked up in the desert in Texas and taken to a prison in McAllen. The judge told me I could never return to the U.S. again or I would spend years in the jail for *migrantes*. I think of this as I huddle under a rock in the freezing rain.

Dozing off, my dreams are of the black beans that Maria knows how to cook, just the way I like them.

Suddenly the "thwack thwack" of a helicopter intrudes on my reveries of home, my Maria, and my children. I am back in hell. Beams of light stab the terrain. "Run for cover!" the *polleros* shout. "It is *la migra*! Run!"

After scrambling to my feet, I grab my backpack and run into the darkness, into the rain-drenched desert that scratches and pricks my skin no matter where I turn. I hear Humberto running beside me, but then I lose him. I am running alone like a rabbit with a pack of hounds on his tail. The helicopter continues to circle our group, eighteen of us running blindly in all directions.

"God help me!" the women scream. We are the hunted, and the hunter shows no mercy. The chopper noise is deafening, the searchlights relentless. I trip and tumble into an *arroyo*. I wonder if I will ever get up again.

But I do. I keep running up the *arroyo*, a riverbed that has some holes that are filling with water. The rain is turning to sleet. Good God, it feels like ice crystals cutting my face. Soon I hear the sound of cars on a nearby road, coming to a stop. There are footsteps somewhere—above me, below me, hard to tell. People running, flashlights on every side of me, piercing the night like shards of glass. The chopper is still circling overhead, creating a wind-storm that thrashes at my body. The icy rain blows into my face and slices my cheek. Small rocks are flying everywhere, making it impossible to see.

I keep going, blindly dodging the beams of light, farther and farther away from the group. Farther from the menacing lights of *la migra*.

I hear the shouts of *la migra* in the distance. "Get down on the ground! Stop running! You are all under arrest!" The orders are in Spanish and English. I keep running and stumbling through the *arroyo*.

As I pull the black garbage bag over my head, making myself invisible in the night, I collapse under a bush. I wait. I claw the ground and dig a little hole, a grave, to hold me on this frozen night. I am an animal, a mole, holding perfectly still. I pant in quiet gasps so I make no noise. Pulling brush and branches over my black plastic cocoon, I pray to God for protection. And I fall asleep.

Waking in the darkness, I hear only the wind and the rain falling around me. No voices, no footsteps. Afraid to move, I take a deep breath and feel a sharp pain in my ribs and groin. Damn *pollero*! I pay him to guide me to Tucson, and this is what I get. Cracked ribs and bruises. But I welcome the silence and feel oddly safe in my little hole. The rabbit has outrun the hounds.

But where am I? Where are my *compadres*?

Dawn breaks. I crawl out of my hole, slowly rising up in the frosty air, shaking the ice crystals out of my hair. There is no one around me. I sit and wait for someone to come walking up this *arroyo*. But no one does. I listen for the chopper. There is nothing. I rub the tiny shards of ice falling from the mesquite branches onto my swollen face and neck. Touching my cheek, I feel dried blood and the scabs from last night's horror.

Afraid to call out for Humberto, I begin walking. The earth is hard and unyielding. I look around me and see mountains, canyons, and rocks. Snow is on top of the bluffs. Ice sparkles in the crevices of rocks. My jacket is stiff with frost. I cannot move my toes. Doing a little dance in the *arroyo*, I start to warm up. I find myself singing a song that my little Juanito learned in school, a song about a dancing frog.

I am a frozen dancing frog on this frigid morning.

And I am alive.

⸻ • ⸻

Looking east at the rising sun, I figure out where to find north. Tucson is north. Nashville is north. I start walking. I see no other members of my group. The women, the men, Humberto—all have vanished. For the first time, I realize that I am alone, totally alone. And I'm on my way to Nashville. To make sushi and to send money back to Maria.

I walk slowly, steadily, staying away from the roads and houses. There are little trails in the desert, perhaps animal trails. Maybe trails of other travelers searching for a job, a family, a warm room. I think about the past three weeks of buses, the train, the dusty roads. Memories of my journey bring a quiet smile to my lips. Slowly trudging through the rocky desert, I recall every day of my journey and feel calm and strong.

The worst days were riding on top of *la bestia,* the beast—the train that brought me north through Mexico. I found a spot on a round tank car, but I was afraid of falling off the train and losing a leg or an arm. I tied myself to a metal bar on the tank car so I wouldn't roll off, using my belt to bind me at the waist. Drinking cans of soda laced with caffeine and swallowing amphetamine pills, I stayed awake for three days.

Thieves prowled the rooftops of the train cars. Several of us on this train car had made a pact when we left Tenosique, a small border town in Tabasco: We vowed that if we were attacked, we would protect each other. We were in this together, like brothers.

In the middle of the night the train slowed down and bandits climbed onto the roof of the car, screaming at me to hand over my money. I didn't move, and I think they thought I was dead or drunk. One kicked me in the back and I almost rolled off, but the belt kept me on the tank car. I pretended to be drunk and unconscious. The guy walked over me and pounded on another guy, looking for money. I tried not to breathe.

During the commotion, my comrades woke up and threatened to throw the bandit off the roof. I prayed to Jesus to keep me alive. I kicked at one of the marauders, and he momentarily lost his balance, pitching toward the edge. Gathering himself up, he moved on. The thieves passed by and harassed the next car of travelers.

I pray right now as I walk through this desert. It is daylight, the sun is warm, and there are puddles of water in the arroyos and rocky basins. My hands and feet are no longer numb. I fill my bottle with water from last night's rain. It looks cleaner than the cow ponds. No cow manure floating in the bottle. The water is reddish from the dirt, and there is grit in my teeth when I drink. But it is cold and sweet. I drink deeply.

I walk, I pray, I collapse under trees. This is how the day goes. I dread nightfall and the cold, empty darkness. In my backpack are two chocolate bars, three dried-up tortillas, and two water bottles. I take two bites of the chocolate and a couple of swallows of water.

After the sun descends behind some mountains, I keep walking until I can no longer see. There is no moon tonight, and the clouds are moving in. More rain, or worse, snow. I see no light from windows, and no other people. I am alone in a desert wilderness.

Like a child, I weep quietly. Then loudly, with huge sobs. Maybe God will hear.

After wrapping my feet in trash bags, I huddle against a rocky ledge to rest. I doze off into a dreamless sleep, but the sounds of snuffling and the clatter of hooves awaken me. Opening my eyes, I can smell the stench of a wild beast. The animal smells like rotted garbage. There is the glint of eyes staring at me and I jump to my feet, grabbing some rocks. Throwing them in the direction of the beast, I see several more of them. They look like huge *puercos*—pigs with hair and huge teeth that snap at the branches and cactus. The herd scatters and their hooves beat in staccato rhythms on the rocky hillside. I toss pebbles and scream at them, but they come back to investigate. I have never seen such animals in Guatemala. There are a couple of babies tagging along with this posse, and the adults are *muy grande*. They are bigger than any pig I have ever seen.

I stand and wave my arms, shouting at them. "Go away! Get lost!" Both fascinated and terrified, I grab my backpack and begin walking in the dark. Am I hiking north or south? Who knows? But I cannot sleep with pigs prowling where I want to rest.

Snow is softly falling and I lift my tongue to the sky. The snowflakes on my face are like the sweet kisses of my children. I begin to cry. I don't know if I am in hell or heaven.

I hear the hooves of the wild pigs on the frozen ground, the clickety clatter of the herd scrambling up a canyon wall. Would it be a sin to kill this animal and eat the flesh? As a Seventh-day Adventist, I do not eat pork. It is unclean and forbidden in the sacred texts of the Bible. However, I would like to club one of the *puercos* with a stick and roast the meat over a fire. I salivate at the thought. God forgive me.

———— • ————

I KEEP WALKING until daylight and see a dim light in the distance. It is a house in the desert. Smoke drifts from the chimney. I can smell the burning mesquite. Aching to be taken in by a kind *americano*, I wait as night changes to day and watch for signs of life inside the house. Of all the things I miss about my Guatemala home, I miss waking up with Maria and my children the most. I watch as the house comes alive. I can hear a radio dispatching the morning news. Children run past a window. Christmas lights twinkle on a tree in the front yard, and a plastic blow-up snowman sits beside a prickly pear cactus. The fake snowman blowing in the wind is the weirdest thing I have ever seen. I wonder if this is an apparition and if I am seeing a white snow ghost. I shake my head and gaze at the ugliness of a plastic red and white snowman, veering and bobbing like a drunken, fat *americano* in the desert. I will never understand the people of this country.

And yet here I am, desperate, hungry and cold, only wanting to make sushi in Nashville. God help me.

I sit quietly, a hundred meters from the house, behind a thicket of sweet-smelling bushes in the wet, misty morning. My hands are bloodied, and the desert grime fills my fingernails. There is a rip in my jeans; my socks are stiff with mud. I wait several minutes, asking God to give me courage. Finally, I approach the house, which is grand with many rooms. Looking in a window, I see a crystal chandelier hanging in the dining room. There are candles on the table. It is early in the morning and I have eaten only a few bites of chocolate and one tortilla in the past twenty-four hours. My stomach growls with hunger. Maybe these *americanos ricos* who have so much can spare a little food. Maybe just some clean water. A banana. I see bananas and oranges in a bowl in the kitchen.

I knock on the door. A woman with blond hair answers in her bathrobe. I smell coffee from the kitchen and something frying and sputtering, like bacon.

"Please, *señora*, do you have any water or food for me? I am lost."

The woman calls to her husband, who comes to the door. He has a cell phone in his hand and is dialing a number. I see a cabinet with a glass door filled with rifles. There is a picture of cowboys and cattle over the cabinet and hunting trophies of deer and antelope on the wall. A fire crackles in the fireplace, and I am transfixed by the warmth and comfort coming from this house in the desert. My knees are weak. I feel like I am going to faint.

"Get the hell off of my property!" the husband shouts. "Get out! Go back to Mexico! Git, now!"

I back away and panic. Holding up my hands like I am under arrest in an American cowboy movie, I plead, "Please, *señor*, no! I will go!"

The man disappears for a moment and comes back with a rifle. He points the rifle at me and again shouts, "Get the hell out of here!"

He does not shoot. Adrenalin rockets through my chest and muscles, and I am scrambling down the driveway, running for my life. My backpack bounces on my back. The mud and rainwater seep into the holes of my shoes, which make a squish sound as I dash down the lane. Running for five minutes, maybe more, I crouch low to dodge any bullets. But there are none.

I look back at the house, and the man is still standing in the doorway with his gun pointed toward me. When I'm out of sight of the house, I collapse to the ground choking and wheezing, trying to calm my breathing. I am shaking and crawl under a bush to rest.

I weep, making animal sounds deep in my throat. I *am* an animal, like the wild pig, and am hated in this land, hunted by the *americanos* in the big fancy houses. I cannot go one more step. My heart pounds wildly in my chest. Breathing rapidly, I close my eyes and pray. I think I fall asleep. When I finally crawl out of my hiding place under the thorny bush, the sun is high overhead.

But I must keep going. There is no work for me in my village. That is certain. When I drive the bus in Guatemala City, the mafia puts the gun to my head and demands five hundred *quetzales* every week. They tell me they will cut off my fingers and then cut out my eyes if I do not pay up. They will go after my Maria and children. My father told me to leave. "Go to *los Estados Unidos* and stay with your sister in Nashville. There is no future here."

How can I work in Guatemala City driving a bus if they take most of my money? I know people who have been killed in the city for just doing their job. They did not have the money for the cartel mafia, who claim to be their protection. Hah! They are men who bow to no one, and they prey upon the poor.

I must keep going.

Three days pass. Maybe four. I cannot count anymore. I just want to sleep.

⸻ • ⸻

December 21, 2013
Juan Carlos

AT DAWN, THE sun shines in my eyes and I wake up. The food is gone. Last night it snowed up to my ankles. Two plastic grocery bags are tied around my feet to keep them dry. When I begin to walk, the bags rip to shreds within minutes. I cannot feel my feet.

I eat the snow and rub it on my face. At times my skin burns, and then I shiver from the cold. I have crossed three ridges of mountains and have seen no one. Not one house since the man pointed a gun at me. Am I back in Mexico? Is this *los Estados Unidos*? I follow the north star at night and walk for a while, then rest. Then the clouds cover the stars and I walk in circles.

I am so thirsty my tongue is like sandpaper and swollen in the back of my throat. It is hard to swallow. I have no more spit. If I sat on this rock all day and ate the snow, it still would not be enough.

It comes to this. I pee in my water bottle and drink it. I gag but keep it down. A couple of coyotes stop and look at me curiously. Their fur is a burnished gold and shines in the sun. They follow me. Do they smell death coming off my skin? Do they smell my stink? They trail me most of the day, or maybe I'm trailing them. I miss them when they leave me. We are a pack, the coyotes and me.

I sink to the ground and can't get up. I sleep. After a while I hear a voice and footsteps, and I sit up and look around. It is the sound of a woman's voice. She tells me to get up. "Move! You cannot lie here underneath this mesquite tree on this cold day of drizzle and ice. Take twenty more steps. You can do this. Get up! Move!"

I see a figure walking quickly by me, then turning and looking into my eyes. It is a woman in a robe of green velvet and stars. She beckons me with her hands and I get up. I can see through her. Then she is gone.

I am going crazy. Crazy is when you see things, no?

Then she appears again. I follow her, and then I see the coyotes again and I follow them. This goes on for most of the day—first the woman, who I come to believe is an angel. A saint perhaps. *La virgen.* Then the coyotes, appearing first in front and then behind. We are all on a quest, an odyssey, a journey into paradise. Or hell. Or worse.

We all continue to walk through the rugged mountains, and I stumble on the rocks. There is absolutely no one to hear my cries of pain, so I scream. My screams echo through the canyons, and I howl until I fall on the ground, exhausted and trembling with tears and terror. The coyotes stop and stare intently at me as I raise my voice to the sky. I rage and wail until I have no voice left. For a while I sleep on a rock in the sun and awaken when the shadows are long and the evening chill sets in.

Rubbing the grit from my eyes, I pick up a walking stick, a stalk from a tall cactus plant, and pull myself up off the rock, steadying my gait. The sun is sinking low in the sky, and soon I am on the edge of a steep canyon. There is water running below, tumbling over rocks, and a house across the crevasse. I am no longer afraid of angry *americanos* and their guns. I do not care. I just need help. Water. Food.

I have never felt so alone. I do not belong anywhere—not here in this strange land of *americanos* who hate me, and not in Guatemala, where there are guns pointed at my head. There is a game I play in my imagination. I sing, I pray, I dream of a house and garden for my family. But the games I play to make myself strong are folly. They no longer work. There is a good chance that I will die here in this foreign land and no one will ever know what happened. I begin to weep again and hate myself for this.

Two dogs are barking across the canyon. The woman in the velvet gown, my desert angel, beckons me to keep moving. She tells me that she will protect me, that I am invisible to all except her. I smell smoke coming out of the chimney of the house. The two dogs are barking nonstop. It is starting to rain lightly again, and I shake my head to make sure this is not a dream, an illusion. I can't tell what is my imagination and what is real.

I walk across a flat meadow toward the edge of the canyon. My walking stick keeps me from stumbling over the slippery rocks. A plastic sack hangs over my shoulders like a *poncho*, and it flaps in the wind.

A woman with white hair comes out of the house and looks at the barking dogs. Then she looks straight at me. Our eyes meet, and we both stand for a moment, just looking at each other. The steep canyon is between us, and I am suspended in time, afraid to move or speak. With each breath, there is pain in my chest.

I fall to my knees and raise my arms to the sky. I cannot go one more step.

Finally I wave to her. "Help me, help me. I am lost. My heart, it is dying." I hold my hand to my chest, I see *la virgen* in the velvet robe motioning to me to follow, and I start to weep.

She walks to the edge of a rock and disappears into the canyon. I think I am crazy. I do not know what is real and what is a fairy tale.

But I am sure those barking dogs are real.

"How do I get across this canyon?" I shout at the woman standing by the house. She is shushing the dogs, but they keep barking.

A man now joins the woman and stands next to her. He points to a place downriver and says it is easier to cross there. He does not have a gun. I think these people are real.

I do not care if he does have a gun. I can go no farther. I will try to cross this steep canyon and ask for food and water. Maybe they will let me rest on their porch for awhile. These are the first people I have seen in days—I do not know how many. I pray they will help me. I cannot spend another night in these mountains, alone in the snow.

When I finally reach the house, I drop to my knees on their patio and try to peel off my plastic garbage sack and backpack. It is difficult to speak. I am too tired to think of words to say, so I say nothing. The woman looks like an *abuela* (grandmother). Her hair is silver, as is her husband's. She approaches me in the drizzle and touches my shoulder. She brushes the wet raindrops off the plastic poncho and helps me lift the drenched sack over my head. I give her my backpack, and she sets it down on the patio. She picks up my water bottle, which is half full of piss, and sniffs it.

I look away.

Opening the door to their home, she invites me in. Her husband nods and gestures for me to enter. I am in a dream.

The house is warm, and a fire glows in the hearth. I walk over and warm my hands near the flames. There are candles and crosses everywhere, and I see a manger scene with Mary and Joseph and the baby Jesus. Music is coming from somewhere, a Christmas hymn.

"Is this a church?"

The woman laughs. "No, this is definitely not a church."

Jesucristo, I have not heard the sound of laughter in weeks.

"You are an angel, and God has put you in my path."

The woman looks puzzled and embarrassed. We both stand by the fire, looking at each other.

I sit on a couch. I am filthy and smell like the pigs. My head is swimming, and I struggle to concentrate on where I am, what I am doing here. I cannot remember how long I have been walking. I cannot remember my sister's name. I breathe deeply and try to do what is right, but I don't know what to do. Slowly I rise from the couch and introduce myself.

"My name is Juan Carlos," I blurt out. "I am lost. I am from Guatemala." My voice is ragged and does not sound like me.

The woman tells me her name is Peg. "Well, actually Margarita." Her *esposo* is Lester. They stare at me, and I cannot stand my smell in this warm, beautiful house. I ask for water. Suddenly she is in a flurry, rushing into the kitchen and bringing me water, tortillas and other food. She gives me hot coffee, and I gulp down the acrid black bitterness, which reminds me of home and Guatemala. I ask for more coffee, and pour in spoonfuls of sugar, enjoying the burning on my tongue.

Suddenly my stomach turns itself inside out and I have vomit in my mouth. Lester quickly shows me the bathroom, and I lose the food in the toilet. I am wet with sweat when I return to the room by the fireplace.

These people, these strangers, disappear into a clothes closet and return with jeans, shoes, and a warm shirt for me. Sniffing at my armpits, I tell Margarita not to approach me. I stink. She returns to the couch with an armload of clean clothes, and a towel with soap.

Lester, the *esposo,* shows me the shower and turns on the hot water. When he leaves the room, I am not sure whether I am alive or dead. Looking in the bathroom mirror, I do not recognize myself. Red dirt fills every line in my face. I am so thin that my pants hang low around my hips. Dried blood and scratches cover my face, arms and legs. I feel dizzy, and then euphoric.

Who are these people who have let me into their house? Are they calling *la migra* now? Will I be in jail tonight? Will they let me stay?

I don't care. I step into the shower and raise my face to the steam. I breathe deeply.

I am alive.

FIVE

═══ • ═══

The Right Thing

Margarita

PEERING OUTSIDE INTO the gathering darkness, I see that it's beginning to snow. I wonder if there are more migrants outside, perhaps soon to be knocking on our door. Is this fellow alone, or is there a group of them waiting in the dark? My mind ricochets from that of being a helping Samaritan to that of a wary guardian of the riches of our life. This man is a stranger, and now he's in the guest bedroom taking a shower. We've known him for thirty minutes.

I look at Lester and tell him to gather up the car and truck keys. Get the check books and credit cards out of sight. Hide the guns. Hide our passports. Hide the coin collection. Hide the turquoise jewelry. I'm in full-blown cautionary mode.

I confess that I was apprehensive when we first settled in this wild place twelve years ago and worried that we would see drug and human traffickers frequently. But we haven't. The migration of people takes place in other parts of the desert where there are known trails and water stations.

My sympathies most definitely lie with the journey of the migrant. I want them to succeed in their search for a life without violence and poverty. The time for immigration reform is way past due, and I am often frustrated with the lack of political movement toward helping the hundreds of thousands of people who are simply seeking connection with their families, or looking for work and a safe place to be.

But this is different. A man has turned up on our doorstep, and I don't know what to do about it. There is no way we can send him on his way. It will be well below freezing tonight. I can't cast him out into the dark and cold on the longest night of the year.

But I am afraid, and this is the bottom line. There are demons that reside in my brain, and they are bringing up the myths, the delusions and the fears of living so close to the Mexican border. As much as I want to welcome this stranger, my doubts are taking hold. I could easily become enmeshed in my anxieties.

Instead, I will cook. I will nourish this man with food. Things always look better on a full stomach. I will prepare comfort food—macaroni and cheese, the leftover tamales, the chips and dips from the holiday party. I put on a CD: classic Bing Crosby crooning "White Christmas." Singing along with Bing, I set to work. Twinkling lights entwine the dead agave plant that is our Christmas tree this year. I light every candle in the living room. We will dine on mac and cheese. I start shredding the cheddar cheese and warming up the milk, flour, and butter for the sauce. It is sustenance on this special, disquieting night.

Eventually, Juan Carlos emerges from the bathroom and he looks better. The clean clothes are a definite improvement. He smells like soap. Both dogs surround him, tails thumping furiously.

I bring my Spanish-English dictionary into the living room and begin to ask questions, struggling with the verbs and the tenses. We pass the dictionary back and forth across the coffee table. He looks up the English words he can't pronounce or remember, and I look up the

Spanish words that have never been needed to converse with a man lost in the desert. We both laugh at our ineptness as we struggle to communicate, and it bonds us. Juan Carlos has a great smile, but I can't tell if he is about to cry when he laughs. The laugh is more like a strangled cough.

His story is confusing and at times contradictory. His sister is in Nashville; then she's living in Texas. Is this another sister? He has been walking from McAllen, Texas. All the way to southern Arizona? I thought he said something about Patagonia. He is talking rapidly in Spanish, three sentences ahead, while I'm stuck on a word he used thirty seconds ago.

It occurs to me that he's in shock and confused about dates, times, places. Acute dehydration, hypothermia, and exhaustion take their toll on the brain cells. His story does not track well. It makes no sense.

Or is he making all of this up? He tells me that one of our neighbors chased him away with a gun. Then he begins talking about being in a Texas prison. Suddenly he holds his face in his hands, stares into space, and talks about sleeping under bushes and under rocks, with wild pigs menacing him at night.

I sit and listen and am not sure what to believe. Lester looks at me and rolls his eyes as if we have a crazy man in our midst.

Arroya and Cassie are curled up asleep at Juan Carlos's feet. The dogs love our unexpected guest. They loved him when he smelled of dung and mud, and they love him now when he smells like Irish Spring soap. Arroya, part Belgian shepherd and God knows what else, demonstrates a particularly shrewd judge of character. She gives you eye contact and intently stares at you to read your face, your mood, your actions. She is coal-black, and has an inquisitive look that scrutinizes and studies your expression. And she always watches your hands. Owing to her deafness, Lester taught her some rudimentary sign language. She's smart as a whip, responding by now to a dozen or more hand commands.

When Juan Carlos entered our house, Arroya was curious about this newcomer with the smells of the desert and the stench of an unwashed human body. But it took just a few pats on her head and a smile from him to win her over. She laid her head on his knee and was softly licking his hand within fifteen minutes.

Cassie looks excited about this newcomer and sniffs his pants, his shoes, his socks. She lays her head on his shoe and looks at me to make sure this is okay. It is. Both dogs are snoring within minutes.

I trust our dogs' judgment more than I do my own. Our hospitality has its limits, but this man is our welcome guest tonight. I begin thinking of him as "J.C." because we are just days before Christmas. *Jesucristo.*

Juan Carlos reaches into the pockets of his discarded jeans, pulling out damp, crumpled pieces of paper. There are phone numbers in smudged, almost illegible scribbles on the scraps, and they flutter to the floor like confetti. Three numbers are missing on one scrap, the lost shred of paper undoubtedly lying in some ditch under an inch of snow. There are damp matches, a throat lozenge, and a prayer card of St. Jude partially ripped in two.

Placing the fragments of paper on the coffee table, Juan Carlos tells me that one of these scraps bears the number of his sister in Nashville. We both stare at the snippets of paper, trying to decipher numbers. It is hopeless.

Finally I ask for his sister's last name, her husband's name, and their address. I call for "information" on the telephone. After several wrong numbers, I find the correct one and dial it. Juan Carlos is excited and eager talk to his sister. The phone rings and rings, but no one answers. We try again. And again. No one answers. There is no answering machine.

Once more I wonder if any of this is true. Is there a sister? Does she live in Nashville? Is Juan Carlos hallucinating? My level of trust goes down; my suspicions about our surprise guest rise up. Maybe Arroya got this one wrong. Is there a sinister streak in this fellow that I haven't detected?

Arroya keeps on snoring. Cassie looks at both of us, sighs, and plops back on Juan Carlos's other foot. Poor J.C. can't move his feet with sixty pounds of dog sprawled across each of his shoes.

Juan Carlos tells me that his sister is Seventh-day Adventist and that since this is Saturday night, she's probably singing in the choir for a special Christmas program. We continue to call every fifteen minutes, and his frustration builds as he listens to the phone ringing endlessly. There's a one-hour time difference, so it's 6 p.m. in Nashville. I figure that if this is the correct phone number, the sister will be home soon.

Meanwhile, we'll have supper. Perhaps the food will help clear some of the confusion about the discordant stories that Juan Carlos is telling us. I place the macaroni and cheese, tamales, and left-over party food on the table, inviting our guest to join us. As I begin to serve the food, I look over at him sitting at our table. His head is bowed in prayer. It is the most intense moment of prayer I have ever witnessed. Both Lester and I wait respectfully, quietly. Juan Carlos's forehead nearly touches the table as he closes his eyes in supplication. It is a silent prayer that goes on for several minutes and I wonder if he's fallen asleep at our table. I count his breaths as he silently sits with bowed head, totally still, deep in prayer. I am humbled and awed by this unabashed moment of faith and reflection. Calling him J.C. makes a lot of sense at this moment.

Christmas candles flicker on this solstice night. The Vienna Boys' Choir sings "O Holy Night" on the CD player. Indeed it is a holy night for all of us.

SIX

Trust

Juan Carlos

I AM OVERWHELMED by the kindness of these *americanos*. Also I am afraid. There is a gun hanging over the door. Maybe they will kill me in the night. At least the black dog likes me. I'm not sure about the yellow one. She is more cautious, more timid.

They did allow me into their home and offered me clean clothes and food. Again I am weeping in the privacy of this bathroom and acting like a baby. I want to talk to Maria and my children to tell them of my good fortune. I am desperate to call my sister, Alma, and I search through my pants to find her phone number. The jeans are filthy, smelling of mud and pigs and piss. Embarrassed, I look for somewhere to toss them, along with my shirt and jacket. These are no longer clothes. They are rags. If I leave them in a heap in the corner, will these kind people throw me out into the cold because I am acting like the wild animals of this desert? Even the dogs smell better than I do.

Lester, the *esposo,* has given me clean jeans and underwear. Holding the clothes to my nose, I inhale the fresh smell of laundry soap and think of home and my wife. What is she doing now? How I would love to speak with her this moment. I shake my head and bring myself back to the present.

I am in a stranger's home and I am alive. I must find my sister. How far is Nashville? Will they make me leave and force me out into the night? I will die if I have to spend one more night under a rock in this hostile land.

Later, sitting in the living room on the couch, the *esposa,* Margarita, looks at the scraps of paper wadded up in my dirty jeans. She picks up the filthy clothes, looks at me for some kind of permission to discard the rags I have been wearing for seven days, and tosses them in the garbage. The stench shames me. But she saves the pieces of paper I had stuffed into my pockets.

She looks upset about the scraps of paper because she cannot read the numbers. I lean forward, straining to understand her English words; she cannot keep up with my Spanish, and I try to slow down. We pass a dictionary back and forth at the coffee table, looking up words, struggling to communicate. She is trying to understand me and flips hurriedly through pages in the dictionary. I am so tired and confused that I cannot remember the things she is asking—how many days in the desert, the address of Alma, the town where I live in Guatemala. She asks for my sister's last name, and Jaime's name too, my brother-in-law. She dials the phone.

I am suddenly afraid she is calling *la migra.*

Exhausted, my mind runs in a thousand directions. I want to rest but must keep going. She wants to know about Nashville, Texas, Guatemala, the journey. I want to lie down and sleep. Finally she is able to get Alma's number from the operator and she hands the phone to me. It rings and rings. Where is she? Has she moved? Why is there no answer?

I remember the first time I came to *los Estados Unidos,* walking, hitchhiking, taking many buses, all the way to Nashville. Working in a Japanese restaurant, I learned another way to cook with raw fish and rice.

Because I wore a red bandanna around my head, people thought I was Japanese. I sent money home, and my family was able to build a bigger house. My father taught in the school. Mama and *Papi* attended the *iglesia evangélica* and told me to find a good church in Nashville. I felt proud of my new skills and the American money I could send home. Every day I prayed to Jesus and would come home smelling like fish and vinegar. I thought of my home in Guatemala and ached to see my family again. After a few years, I did return. My mother was sick, but I think her sickness was worry and sadness for me. She recovered quickly when I arrived back in our village.

The second time I crossed into *los Estados Unidos*, I was chased by *la migra* after floating on an inner tube across the Rio Grande. From the banks of the river, my companions and I hid in the bushes and then walked for two days before being spotted. I was caught and spent many weeks in jail in McAllen, Texas, before I was sent back to Guatemala. I was so ashamed of having been caught that I stayed away from my village for weeks before returning to my father. I don't know which was worse: being captured by *la migra* or facing my father. My family had saved up so much money to pay the *coyote* guide, and I had failed them.

Now I sit in a stranger's house in a place called Arizona. My head hurts and my stomach is telling me to eat, and then it tells me not to eat. I ask Margarita what day is today, and it is Saturday. Ah, church day. No wonder there is no one at home. Alma is singing in church for the Seventh-day Adventist Christmas program. In *los Estados Unidos*, Alma's church celebrates this holiday called Christmas. We do not do this kind of Christmas celebrating with music and gifts in my village. My sister has taken on the customs of her new home in America.

I must reach Alma. She will get me a ride to Nashville. I have come so close to my destination. Please, God, let Alma answer the phone.

Still there is no answer.

Margarita wants to serve the food for supper. My stomach feels empty, and I look at the noodles and tamales. I am afraid that I will throw up the food again. The house is so peaceful and beautiful, they will toss me out into the cold if I vomit on the table. Sitting here, I see candles and hear music. Again I ask if this is a church. She smiles and says no, it is just the time of Christmas.

I wonder if I am dead and this is heaven.

Overwhelmed with gratitude and longing for home, I bend my head in prayer, hiding my tears as best I can. I hold my rumbling stomach, which aches for food but is topsy-turvy. My head touches the table and my arms hold my stomach. I pray to Jesus for strength and courage because I am a coward. I do not want to face the desert and the mountains again. Please let me just stay here in this place and sleep by the fire. Maybe these people will allow me to stay. I will sweep the floor, I will clean the toilets, I will do anything to stay inside the warmth of this house.

And please keep me from throwing up at the table.

Amen.

Margarita places the macaroni and cheese on my plate and serves me the tamales and corn. I eat everything quickly and drink more coffee. I cannot get enough coffee. It is the drink I miss most, the coffee of the Guatemala highlands. The macaroni is fragrant with the *queso*, and I marvel at the thick creamy sauce and melted strings of cheese. It has been so long since I had a supper like this.

Suddenly the nausea hits me again, slamming me in the gut. Cold sweat covers my face, and I push away from the table and race to the bathroom. I'm on my knees hanging over the toilet. Everything comes up. The acid secretions burn my throat, and I cannot breathe. Weak and dizzy, I collapse on the cold tile floor and lie there for several minutes. I want to lie here all night.

I do not know how long I am on the floor, but eventually I get up and go back to the dining table. Margarita looks concerned and holds my wrist, checking my pulse. She tells me she is an *enfermera,* a nurse. She takes away the plate of food. "I will fix some chicken soup," she says.

I smile briefly. My mouth tastes like vinegar and salt. I have no idea what she is saying.

I ask if we can try to call my sister again, and we do this again and again. Still no answer. After leaving the table, I lie down on the couch by the fire. I want to stay here in case we are able to reach Alma on the phone. I drift off and dream of angels and pigs and tortillas.

SEVEN

―――― • ――――

Connection

Margarita

JUAN CARLOS STRETCHES out on the couch and I cover him with a blanket. He looks pale and exhausted, and his breathing is deep and steady. He is asleep in minutes, looking almost beatific. I don't know how old he is. I don't know his last name. And he is asleep on my couch in front of the fireplace.

I continue to call the number in Nashville, but the phone rings endlessly. I wonder if Juan Carlos is imagining all of this. Does he have a sister? Is he really from Guatemala? Who is this person asleep on my couch? Can I trust him?

My husband reminds me that he is making no sense. First he tells us he has a sister in Nashville. Then in Texas. The crumpled bits of paper lie in tatters on the coffee table, the penciled numbers barely legible. Is this even the right number? No one has answered. Maybe his sister has moved.

I call the number every fifteen minutes. It's midnight in Nashville when someone finally answers the phone. Speaking in Spanish, a woman's voice is soft and questioning. I hear activity and children in the background.

"*¿Es esta Alma?*" I ask.

"*Me llamo Margarita. Vivo en Arizona.*" My name is Margarita. I live in Arizona.

"Juan Carlos, your brother, is in my home in Arizona."

There is a long pause.

"*Mi hermano está en Arizona?*" (My brother is in Arizona?) she says and begins to cry. She hands the phone to a man who speaks English. I assume it's her husband, Jaime. In the background I hear excited voices, screeches and cries. I look over at the couch where Juan Carlos is softly snoring and tell Jaime that J.C. is safe and sound asleep. We decide to talk again in the morning and come up with a plan for transporting our weary guest.

⟹ • ⟸

STOKING THE FIRE, Lester and I retire to our bedroom, shutting the door. Arroya stays with Juan Carlos, sleeping soundly beside the couch, her head propped on J.C.'s hand on the cushions. Cassie is restless and nervous about the stranger in our midst and paces about our bedroom, unsure about where to settle down for her long winter's nap.

Lester and I don't settle down either, and my mind is moving along a dozen circuitous paths. We both lie in bed, eyes wide open, wondering what to do next. Our home is seventy miles from Tucson. Drawing a map to Tucson, packing some food in a backpack and sending J.C. on his way is out of the question. It's December, and the temperatures are below freezing at night.

We're both wary and suspicious about this stranger asleep on the couch. What if he attacks us in the night? We still don't know his last name. My incompetence in ascertaining such basic information slams me with self-doubt.

I tell Lester we should wake up our guest and take him to the *casita*—our guest house—which is separate from our home. The plain fact of the matter is that I'm uncomfortable sleeping in the same house with Juan Carlos. I don't know who this person is, or whether he would harm us in any way. Having read too many books about Ciudad Juárez and the carnage of that traumatized city, I can't get the images of mayhem and violence out of my mind. Juan Carlos seems like a nice fellow, but who the hell knows?

Tonight I am driven by fear and suspicion.

I walk back into the living room where Juan Carlos is sound asleep. I gently wake him, and Arroya licks his hand. J.C. is startled awake and looks at me quizzically.

"Did you call my sister?" he asks.

"Yes, and she will call us in the morning so we can decide what to do."

"Can you drive me to Tucson? Alma can arrange for a ride to Nashville." J.C.'s eyes are pleading.

"I can't drive you to Tucson because there is a checkpoint with *la migra* between here and the city. We will both go to jail."

"Is it morning?" J.C. shakes his head awake and looks out the window into the black night. It's softly snowing, and the desert is silent and forbidding. The Christmas lights on my desert holiday tree are the only lights in the room.

"No, it's only eleven at night. Lester and I would like you to sleep up in our *casita* tonight. You will be more comfortable there." My gaze shifts around the room. I'm clearly unsettled about asking him to move. I am uneasy, circling this man on the couch like a mountain lion. I realize I want him out of my house. At least for tonight. I need space and time to think.

J.C. looks at me with a puzzled expression. He pulls the blanket up over his chin and stares at the fire. "I am very comfortable here, and besides, Alma may call again and I want to talk to her. Please. I am very comfortable here." There is a mix of pleading and bullheadedness in his voice.

I look him straight in the eye.

"Juan Carlos, I think it is best if you sleep in the *casita*. Lester will walk you to the place where our guests sleep. It is warm and safe there. Alma won't call again. It's after midnight in Nashville."

I feel like a stern mother telling her children they must trudge up the stairs and turn off the TV set. They must do it my way. I hate asking J.C. to move to the *casita*, but I'm full of fear and uncertainty. At this moment I am a coward.

J.C. looks confused and forlorn. He is clearly exhausted. Slowly, he gets up from the couch and looks at us awkwardly. Lester and I gather his things and we walk him to the door. Arroya and Cassie are delighted with a late night walk in the snow and jump around with glee, tails wagging.

It's settled. Juan Carlos will sleep in the *casita* tonight, and we will come up with a plan in the morning. When Lester and J.C. walk out the door, I feel better immediately. And guilty. And paranoid. My stomach is in a knot. Worried about the web I've created, I realize I have no idea what I'm doing.

Except I will get a good night's sleep, and in the morning we will talk with Alma and her husband in Nashville. At least I know they exist. That's the first step.

EIGHT

═══ • ═══

Hope

Juan Carlos

I CAN'T UNDERSTAND why they are kicking me out of their home
at midnight. First they invite me to sleep on the couch by the fire. Now
they want me out, and Lester is walking with me to a small *casita* far
from the house. Do they think I am a thief? Are they going to call *la
migra*?

I beg Margarita, "Please, may I stay on the couch by the fire with the
black dog? I feel safe here, and for the first time in weeks I am warm. I
want to be here if Alma calls again."

Margarita tries to assure me, but her words are hollow. "Alma will talk
to you in the morning. We will figure out a way to get you to Nashville."
She gathers up my backpack and the clean clothes, stands by the door,
and waits for me to leave. I am stunned and afraid, but I have no choice.

Slowly, I trudge up to the *casita*, which is separate from the house.
Lester does not say anything, and he doesn't understand my questions
anyway. He doesn't speak Spanish. I stumble through some phrases in
English, trying to understand why I am being sent to the *casita*. "You
will be fine in the casita," Lester says. "I'll show you where the heater

is." We both laugh a little as the dogs jump and frolic in the frosty night. The dogs, the quiet beauty of this night, Lester's calm nature—all of these things help me relax.

There are a few snowflakes falling, and the desert is ghostly quiet. I cannot see the stars, as the sky is iron gray. The snow feels like feathers on my cheek. As I walk with the black dog by my side, I try not to cry.

There is a bed, shower and toilet in the *casita*, and the heater is on. The room is comfortable. A blanket with a picture of *la Virgen de Guadalupe* is on the bed, and my eyes spill over with tears. Turning my head away, I try not to show my sadness and fear. Lester shows me the little kitchen, the dishes, the extra blankets if I need them. He says something I do not understand, but his eyes are kind, and I relax for a moment.

The black dog wants to stay with me, but Lester insists that the dog return with him to the big house. I have never felt so close to a dog before. I love this black dog, and I am sure she loves me.

As soon as Lester leaves, I am on my knees praying to God for help. I am alone, bone-weary, and afraid.

But Alma answered the phone! Margarita assured me that Alma will talk to me in the morning. My sister will help me. Collapsing onto the bed with all of my clothes and jacket still wrapped around me, I begin to weep. I shiver uncontrollably and hug myself like a child. In minutes I am asleep.

Morning. I am lying on the bed, and sunlight streams through the windows. Sometime during the night I pulled the thick blankets over me. I am warm, curled up like a contented cat. So what do I do now? Do I stay here until Margarita comes and gets me? Is *la migra* on the way? At this moment I do not care.

I am utterly and totally at the mercy of these people in the big house on the edge of the cliff. Maybe I should just run now. But where? And then there is Alma. I must talk to her. If only I can convince these people to keep me here until my family comes for me.

A knock on the door startles me out of my thoughts. It is Lester and he asks me to come to the big house for breakfast. He smiles and beckons me to follow, and I do. The black dog, Arroya, greets me and leads the way to the house. She looks behind her every few steps to make sure I am following. Her pink tongue hangs halfway out of her mouth, and she looks like she is smiling. As we enter the house, the smell of fresh coffee welcomes me. Margarita is cheerful in her apron, inviting me to sit. "*Siéntase, por favor,*" she says as she pours me a mug of coffee. Sun fills the room, providing a welcome glow after last night's snowfall. The surrounding hills are covered with a dusting of snow, and I take in a deep breath, grateful that I was not sleeping in the frigid dampness last night.

Something pulled me toward this house yesterday. I shake my head awake and wipe away thoughts of dying under a rock, with the wild pigs and coyotes licking my bones. My mind wanders off and I cannot control where it goes. My imagination whips and bends like a snake I saw a few days ago, going to places I do not want to face. One minute I am alert, the next minute I feel confused and dizzy.

But I am here, holding a steaming cup of coffee. This is real. Margarita makes the coffee strong too, just like home. I sniff the bitter brew and ask for sugar, *por favor.* I must focus on this moment. I scoop up four spoonfuls of sugar, and I notice Margarita staring at me as I stir the sugary sweetness into my coffee. She looks perplexed as my spoon clinks against the cup and the sugar dissolves. Margarita pours milk in her own cup of coffee. No sugar.

"The sugar will give me energy! ¡Fuerte!" I flex my muscles and give a weak smile.

Margarita dials the number of my sister and hands me the phone. I feel like this is all a miracle—the coffee, the food, the sunlight, and now my sister crying on the phone from Nashville. She is telling me she loves me. Alma and her husband, Jaime, want to know where this house is located so they can arrange for transportation. I give the phone to Margarita and sit with my coffee, staring out at the mountains. Rainbow colors dance off the droplets of ice on the trees. I know this will be a good day.

NINE

The Plan

Margarita

I SPEAK WITH Alma for a moment, but soon I am talking with
Jaime, her husband. I try to explain the remoteness of our location, and
the fact that transporting J.C. anywhere is a federal offense that could
land us all in jail. We talk about alternate possibilities.

Maybe J.C. could walk to the freeway and be picked up. Of course,
it is fifteen miles to the freeway, and the desert is unforgiving this time
of year. Someone would probably spot him. Plus, I doubt if he's strong
enough to walk that far.

I hear Alma's rapid-fire Spanish in the background, and children's
chatter interrupting the conversation. There are sounds of weeping, and
I sense that Alma is frantic about getting help for her brother. Jaime
remains calm on the phone with me, and we hash out some possibilities for a rendezvous.

Our house is many miles from the major highway to Tucson. Even
our neighbors have difficulty finding us because many of the roads are
unmarked. I try to explain where we're located, and realize that it is
hopeless. There are too many rural roads; providing directions over
the phone just leads to confusion. We decide to talk later. Jaime tells

me they will find a driver—a friend of the family—who will transport J.C. to Nashville. But they need time to arrange this.

"Do you mean you will send a person who knows how to transport Juan Carlos to Nashville?" I ask.

"Yes," replies Jaime. "We have a good friend who does this kind of thing."

Is Jaime speaking of a human smuggler? Immediately I'm gripped with trepidation about dealing with such a person, but I can't think of any other options at this point.

"I will send you money for all of your help," Jaime adds.

"No, please, I don't want any money," I tell him repeatedly. "We will take care of J.C. and figure out a plan of transportation for him."

Jaime is insistent about sending me money. I am equally adamant about refusing it. We go back and forth about this. In my mind, money just makes this whole episode nefarious. Plus, this is not a business transaction. This is a rescue mission.

I need to come up with a plan that will get J.C. to Tucson, where he can then get a ride on to Nashville. This means getting through the checkpoint, a station set up by Immigration Customs and Enforcement (ICE), between our house and Tucson. All cars must pass through this checkpoint, which is twenty miles from the border on a major freeway to Tucson. Border Patrol vehicles constantly patrol our region, looking for undocumented migrants who they claim are on a rampage of killing, robbing, smuggling, and trafficking drugs.

I look at Juan Carlos, who is unarmed and physically depleted after days alone in the desert. The whole business of thousands of migrants pillaging and killing is absolutely ludicrous. Criminalizing a person who is lost and fleeing from his home country because of a crumbling government that cannot protect its people—well, this is vicious and immoral. We will figure out a way for J.C. to reach his destination.

TEN

Faith

THERE IS NO doubt in my mind that my country has an insatiable appetite for forbidden fruit—marijuana, cocaine, heroin, opioids, and methamphetamines. Mexico and Central America have the product, and we are ready to buy at whatever is the going rate. The "War on Drugs" is without question a colossal failure. Illicit drugs are cheaper, more plentiful, and easier to get now than they were forty years ago. I'm told the quality is better, too. My countrymen get their highs on the backs of Latino migrants who are willing to risk their lives carrying a load of drugs. All of this mayhem so our fellow citizens can feed their addictions.

In America during the 1850s and 1860s, there was the Underground Railroad, smuggling slaves to the North. In Europe during World War II, there was also human smuggling as brave citizens in many countries hid and saved many Jews. Today I am hiding a man from Guatemala instead of a Jew or a slave from Africa. I am trying to figure out how to circumvent the Border Patrol agents and get this man to his family, to a job, to relative safety. I've never broken the law before, certainly not in a premeditated, plotting, scheming sort of way. The whole idea makes me nauseated. It's frightening, but also strangely exciting.

This is not some article out of *Mother Jones* about social justice. This is the real deal. I will be meeting with a human smuggler in possibly twenty-four hours. If there is another way to get J.C. to Tucson, it doesn't cross my mind at this moment.

I serve breakfast and don't eat a bite.

═══ • ═══

Margarita

WHEN I ASK Juan Carlos about the drugs and the migrants, he tells me that a few in his group carried burlap sacks of marijuana.

"I never carried the drugs, but others in my group did."

He doesn't know what happened to the contraband or the men who were carrying the load. When the helicopters and the Border Patrol descended on his group, there was chaos.

There is a reduction in the price you must pay the *coyote* guides if you're willing to be a drug mule and carry the cargo. I ask if anyone in his group of eighteen used any of the drugs and he laughs. It's the first time I've seen him laugh.

"The Americans are the only ones that can afford the drugs. We just carry them. The drugs are your thing."

I remember the weed I smoked back in the 1960s, never thinking about how the baggies of pot made their way into my life, into my hands. The marijuana was from Mexico and was a welcome respite on my days off as a nurse living in San Francisco. My circle of friends would pass a joint of potent weed around, along with a bottle of cheap red wine. The transport and marketing of marijuana on the backs of Latinos never entered my mind.

Juan Carlos asks for a broom and offers to sweep the floor. It's littered with dog hair, dead leaves and muddy paw prints. Handing him the broom, I'm embarrassed about the dirt on the floor and the clutter on every flat surface in the room.

"Can I stay here for a while and work for you? I can help you here. I can scrub your floors, clean your bathrooms, and help Lester with building projects."

The thought terrifies me. The idea of hiding our migrant friend here for several days is dangerous. J.C. reads my face and sees the fear. It's the Christmas season, and there will be many people coming and going in and out of our house. The idea just won't work. I imagine myself locked up in a jail cell for harboring a fugitive.

"It's too dangerous, Juan Carlos. We must get you to Nashville safely." Arroya licks J.C.'s hand. She likes his company.

I make the decision to transport Juan Carlos to a remote rural road that can easily be found by the family friend/human smuggler. Hoping that his family connection in Nashville is already making this arrangement, I call Alma to check their progress. I plot a rendezvous meeting point at a freeway exit that's often deserted, but easily found on a map.

Jaime answers when I call, and we decide to meet the smuggler at noon the following day, December 23. I give detailed instructions to Jaime, and he relays this information to a driver who will meet us at the specified location. I explain that I'll park near some bushes by a railroad track until I hear from the smuggler, or the "family friend." Then the transfer of Juan Carlos into a waiting car can be made. Giving my cell phone number to Jaime, I'm suddenly seized with fear about a stranger—a smuggler, perhaps—having access to my private contact information. I put it out of my mind.

After hanging up the phone, I talk with Juan Carlos about the plan. His face looks both elated and relieved, and he clasps my hands in gratitude. He's close to tears, while I'm feeling a combination of relief and anxiety. And guilt.

To be honest, I don't want the burden of hiding this man in my house. And I'm extremely apprehensive about transporting him to some

unknown person in the middle of the day in broad daylight at a hope-
fully deserted freeway exit. Often there are Arizona Highway Patrol,
Border Patrol, and National Guard vehicles patrolling the borderlands.
The militarization of southern Arizona is a fact of life to which local
residents have begrudgingly acquiesced. Roadway checkpoints, dogs
sniffing at your tires, questions about citizenship, Border Patrol agents
giving chase and running after young men in dark hoodies—these are
things I occasionally see when driving into town.

Lester and I devise a plan: I will transport Juan Carlos alone. He'll
sit in the back seat of our car and crouch on the floor when other cars
approach. If a police officer or Border Patrol agent stops me, I will tell
them that I'm a nurse and that I have a man in the back seat who is
gravely ill. I'm on my way to the emergency room at the local hospital
in Nogales. If the officer wants to follow me, fine.

All true.

If I'm not stopped, I will wait for the smuggler and transfer Juan
Carlos into the vehicle as planned, after which he'll somehow make it
to Tucson and then on to Nashville. I consider driving J.C. to Nashville myself, or meeting his family half-way, but I would need to get
him past the checkpoint that is on the route to Tucson, and I don't
know how to do that.

I draw a map with landmarks to Tucson in case the smuggler aban-
dons Juan Carlos—a frequent occurrence in the deadly game of human
migration. On a scrap of paper, I draw the Santa Cruz River, the railroad tracks, the checkpoint he must avoid, and the towns between
here and Tucson.

I think about what a preposterous scheme this is. It'll never work.
And yet somehow thousands of Latinos make it through all the bar-
riers every year.

I find a backpack in the closet and fill it with energy bars, cheddar
cheese, canned smokey joe wieners, corn chips, a rain poncho, and

bottles of water. Lester gives J.C. a watch. We find a wool army jacket, a fleece shirt, jeans, a belt, clean socks, gloves, and a warm hat. I wish I could give him a cheap cell phone, but the nearest store where I might find one is more than an hour away.

Juan Carlos spends the rest of the day quietly relaxing, walking around the ranch, and mentally preparing for the journey. "Can I take the dog with me?" he asks at one point. "I will look more like an American walking my dog." Arroya looks at him adoringly.

Lester is horrified by the suggestion, and I explain that, no, Arroya is a part of our family and we couldn't part with her.

"Do you have any gel for the hair?" he asks. "Do you have hair clippers? I want to cut my hair."

Puzzled by this question, I find some sharp scissors, and Juan Carlos retires to the bathroom and snips at his hair. I can hear the snip-snip-snip and am mildly annoyed that he's so concerned about his appearance when there are real dangers to contemplate and strategies to discuss. He comes out of the bathroom with a ragged, uneven haircut, looking worse than before. He looks like a punk rocker. If moths had nibbled at his hair, they would have done a better job.

With the stubby snippets of coal-black hair scattered erratically over his head, he would stand out on most streets in America. Juan Carlos is a stranger in an inhospitable land. Hair gel and a dog accompanying him on his journey are not going to change his image. Hiding in the shadows is the only way he'll make it to Tucson.

I glance over toward Juan Carlos, and he is on his knees beside our couch, his head once again bowed in prayer. Arroya is beside him, looking quizzically at her new friend, a whisper of a tail wag attending her gaze as she watches his lips move in silent petition to the gods of the desert.

Profoundly moved by this man's unabashed demonstration of faith, I watch for a moment and then avert my eyes and say my own prayers. I pray for myself; I do not want to go to jail. I pray for Juan Carlos; I want him to arrive in Nashville and reunite with his sister. I pray that there will be no Border Patrol agents on the road to the freeway where we will meet the smuggler who will drive Juan Carlos to safety. I pray that the smuggler is a good person and will not harm my passenger or me. I pray that this is not the dumbest thing I have ever done in my life.

I pray like a child, asking for the gift of safety for my friend and myself. And I pray that it will suddenly be two weeks from now and that all will be well. At this moment there is nothing sophisticated or esoteric about my petition to God.

Frightened about this whole business because I'm a coward, I pray for calm in my own private storm. Looking out the window, I see shards of sunlight piercing through the storm clouds and take this to be a sign of positive things to come. As the day wears on, I visualize J.C. in a car heading north, cruising into Nashville in two days, and his sister preparing a feast of chicken and black beans and thick corn tortillas, the kind that fill you up for hours.

Quietly, the hours pass. I wrap family Christmas presents. Juan Carlos naps on the couch. Arroya sleeps on the rug beside him. Cassie snores nearby in front of the fire. Lester watches a football game on the TV in another room. I say a silent prayer that the neighbors won't drop by for a holiday visit.

Daylight begins to falter at four o'clock, and the room takes on a blue cast in the winter's evening light. It begins to look like it may snow again, and there is a soft drizzle on the desert floor. The birdseed in the feeders is soggy, looking moldy. I long for the iconic dry heat and sunshine of Arizona. This feels more like Chicago, cold and dismal and wet.

Juan Carlos would not have survived another night in this weather. We're doing the right thing. There will be snow in the mountains tonight. I'm sure of it.

Taking a deep breath, I tell myself that we will get through this chapter. We have food, shelter, a warm fire, and we are safe. For now.

ELEVEN

---•---

Hunted

Juan Carlos

I REJOICE WHEN I talk with Alma on the phone. She sounds so close! Why can't these Americans hide me in their car and drive me to a place where we can meet Alma and Jaime, close to Nashville? Praise be to God that Jaime is arranging for a driver to pick me up and carry me to safety. I am so afraid that I will do something wrong, something disrespectful, and the *americanos* will tell me to leave. They are so kind and yet there is fear behind their eyes. Are they afraid of me?

I confess, I am still not sure I trust them. Will they call *la migra* and try to get rid of me? Every time Margarita picks up the phone, I figure she's calling *la migra*.

My stomach is still on fire and I'm having trouble eating the strange food. I long for Maria's cooking and do not want to insult Margarita. Nothing appeals to me right now, but I must build up my strength for the journey ahead.

"Do you have any honey?" I ask. "Honey will give me energy and make me strong. ¡*Fuerte!*" I puff up my chest and flex my muscles. Margarita searches through her cupboards but can't find any. I miss the honey from the hives in the trees in Guatemala.

I hope I do not vomit at the table tonight, but my stomach is right on the edge. How can I be so hungry and yet feel sick after I eat? I must try. All I want to do is sleep in front of this fire. I will lie down on the couch and try to sleep. It is getting late in the afternoon. I hope they do not send me up to the *casita* tonight. I want to stay here beside the fire with the dogs.

Dinner goes well. Margarita prepares chicken soup with vegetables and noodles, and there are tortillas, but not the thick corn tortillas of Guatemala. No matter. I devour everything, including some tamales. My stomach feels sick and rumbles, but the food stays down. I am getting stronger and am preparing for whatever happens tomorrow. God has placed these *americanos* in my path, and I will not disappoint Him.

I look around the room at the candles, the tiny Christmas lights on the tree, and the crackling logs in the fireplace. Closing my eyes, I think about my family. What would they think of me sitting at this fine table with the *americanos*? Maybe my life can be like this someday. Warm, secure, plenty of food, and my family around me.

After dinner, I am alone by the fireplace. Curling up on the couch, I pull a blanket over me, a blanket with a design of *la Virgen de Guadalupe* printed in bold colors. I dream of angels and fire and wild pigs and my sister. When I wake up it is dawn, and I have not moved from this couch all night. The black dog, Arroya, is snoring on the floor beside me. Lester tells me that the dog cannot hear.

How can a dog survive without ears to hear?

How can a man from Guatemala who works in the *campos* (fields) picking coffee beans survive a journey in the desert and find his way to Nashville? With God's help, the dog will live a good life in this house, and I will be cooking noodles and fashioning beautiful designs of sushi in Nashville.

Morning comes, and the fire is down to glowing embers. The smell of mesquite fills the room. If only I could stay here and work for this family. They need help with the landscaping. I see dog hair everywhere inside the house. I could live in the *casita* away from the house and figure out a way to get to Nashville. I need to get stronger and rest.

But the plan is in place. We will meet a driver who will take me to safety tomorrow. Alma and Jaime assure me that this is the best strategy. They are prepared to pay the driver to deliver me to safety.

Margarita is in the kitchen preparing coffee and breakfast, and I savor the warmth of the brew. Stepping outside holding a steaming cup, I bask in the sunshine. Snow speckles the mountaintops and ice crystals appear on the bare branches, projecting blinding reflections of colors that dance in the light. I look around the wilderness across the canyon where I walked just a few days before. The rocks and the canyon river are forbidding and achingly beautiful. There are no houses visible at this ranch. It is the perfect place for me to stay and recover from my days in the desert. I do not want to leave, but Margarita is determined to deliver me to a driver, a person who knows how to transport me to Tucson and the next phase of my journey.

It is time to leave this refuge. Both dogs kiss my face before I climb into the car. Margarita asks me to sit in the back seat and crouch down when we drive off the ranch. After saying good-bye to Lester and my new friend Arroya, who has not left my side, I climb into the car.

When a car approaches on a deserted road, I get on the floor. I feel like a hunted animal hiding from menacing lions that pace just outside the car door. My heart is beating inside my chest like the drums of *los indios* from my village, and I can hardly breathe. After a moment, Margarita tells me I can sit up in the seat, but I am afraid. I do not want to be captured, and so I stay curled up like a cowardly kitten on the back floor of the car. I feel shame and terror and gratitude all at once. Margarita reaches her hand into the back seat and I feel her patting my shoulder as I am crouched on the floor.

"It's okay," she says. "You are going to be okay. Everything is okay."

She is speaking to me, but I am not listening. Forcing my breaths to slow down, I try to calm myself. Margarita can probably hear the beating of my heart as it races inside my chest. Praying for peace within me, I begin to weep. I must regain control of myself.

After thirty minutes of driving, we stop at our destination, the place by the railroad tracks. I stay on the floor of the car, and Margarita tells me she does not see any other vehicles close by. We wait here for several minutes. It is noon, the time of our meeting with the driver, but no one has appeared.

We wait fifteen minutes. Margarita calls Nashville and Alma answers. She hands the phone to me, and I tell Alma we are at the meeting place but there is no one here. Alma tells me to hang up and she will check with the driver, the smuggler, on her phone and call us back.

We wait in the car, and I am still crouched on the floor in the back seat. Margarita is parked at the side of the road. Many cars pass by. A few are Border Patrol vehicles. She tells me to stay on the floor. I am sweating one moment and shivering the next. It is now 12:30 p.m., and still no driver has appeared to pick me up.

Margarita calls Nashville again on her cell phone and hands me the receiver. Jaime answers and tells me that the driver can see us but does not want to be seen. He tells me to step out of the car when there are no other vehicles on the road, and wait in the bushes close to the railroad tracks.

I hand the phone back to Margarita and hear her ask to speak with the smuggler. She is asking for the smuggler's phone number. The smuggler refuses to give it to her.

"Well, tell the driver to call me so I understand where I should drop off Juan Carlos." Margarita is insistent about how the transfer should take place.

After she hangs up, we wait for several minutes, and soon her cell phone rings. It is the man who will guide me to safety and connect me with a ride to Nashville, *gracias a Dios*. She asks the driver where she should deliver me.

"I don't understand," I hear her say. "Where should I drop off Juan Carlos?"

When she hangs up, she tells me that there are thick bushes by the railroad tracks close to the road, and that is the place where my smuggler, my savior, will find me.

"Stay down for a few minutes," she says. "There are Border Patrol agents driving by." Her voice cracks and is full of fear.

Margarita puts her hand on my shoulder in the back seat as I lie curled up on the floor and tells me when to get up and get out of the car. She asks me something, but I am praying and do not hear her words. My prayer is simple: "Help me."

"Are you okay about doing this?" she asks again.

I tell her yes, but my heart is shouting no. I am terrified.

"You are going to be okay," she says. "You are strong and your family is waiting for you in Nashville. If the driver doesn't come, you have a map. You have my phone number. Walk north to Tucson."

She gives me a handful of American dollars in case I need to buy more food or water.

"I will not forget you. Call me when you get to Nashville. *Vaya con Dios.*"

Finally, after several more moments, she opens the car door and I squint in the sunlight. It is early afternoon and I run into a bramble of bushes and twigs. I see no one. After Margarita pulls away, I watch her car disappear in the distance.

I wait. I look at the watch that Lester gave me. I sit in the bushes and peer around this lonely spot. Cars rush by. Some of them are Border Patrol and police cars.

HOURS PASS. AT three o'clock it starts to rain softly, and the sunlight is fading. It is cold and wet and gray; I shiver as the drops trickle down my neck. Where is this driver? Where is my ride to Tucson? I can't call Alma. I can't call Margarita. I have no phone and I am alone in this place watching the cars go by. I long for the warm fire and the black dog. My muscles ache from crouching in the bushes for so long.

At five o'clock I realize that there is no one to deliver me from this place in the bushes. It is almost dark and I must decide what to do. I will start walking north to Tucson, following the railroad tracks and the river. I must begin moving or I will freeze.

Margarita called the river the Rio Santa Cruz. It is a holy name. I will not die beside a river with such a holy name.

Looking repeatedly at my watch, I walk three hours and I rest three hours. I take shelter at a rotting wooden shed that is leaning to one side. Sitting in a corner on the ground, I doze. It is dark and the rain is softly falling, dripping through the cracks in the roof. One moment I am shivering, teeth rattling. The next moment I am damp with sweat, my head throbbing.

Margarita has given me some aspirin and I quickly swallow a few. Soon I am dozing, curled up in a ball, the damp earth seeping through my jeans. I dream of a warm fire and a black dog.

Startled awake by a snuffling noise, I see a cow curiously nosing around my backpack, which smells of tortillas and cheese. The cow has the biggest set of horns I have ever seen. I shout a curse at this intruder and the cow jumps away in fright. Shaking my head awake, I get up and see in the dim light a herd of cattle staring at me, entering this lean-to out of curiosity. Even the cows seek warmth and company.

I begin my walk toward Tucson, watching for other migrant travelers, hoping I will meet someone on this darkest of nights. There is absolutely no one on this trail by the river. No lights, no human beings.

I am utterly alone.

TWELVE

Free Fallin'

Margarita

DRIVING AWAY FROM the drop-off site, I leave Juan Carlos in the bushes by the railroad tracks. I feel immense relief. My hands shake and my heart pounds, elated that I wasn't caught by the Border Patrol agents and other police vehicles cruising the area. The plan has gone smoothly. There were a thousand things that could have gone wrong, but luck was on our side. No arrests, no one stopping me for questions. Three, maybe four Border Patrol vehicles cruised by while I was waiting for that phone call from the smuggler. I was sure one of them would stop and ask if I was having car trouble. As a precaution, I held my cell phone to my ear, pretending I'd pulled over to the side of the road and was having a conversation, a common practice at this freeway exit.

Still fearful of being caught in a trap by either the smuggler or Border Patrol agents, I take some deep breaths and try to calm down. My mind had raced with fleeting fears of both of us being kidnapped or extorted for money by the human smuggler. And I was panic-stricken about being arrested for transporting an undocumented person. Bravery is not my strong suit today. Neither of these scenarios played out, and I am relieved and on the edge of tears.

I'm still shaking several minutes after speaking with the smuggler. He spoke calmly with a Spanish accent and seemed both patient and competent on the phone. First he gave Juan Carlos directions in Spanish and then he spoke with me in perfect English.

"Just leave Juan Carlos beside the railroad track," he said. "The bushes will act as a cover. I will pick him up after you drive away. I don't want to draw attention to our activity."

The smuggler made it clear that he didn't want me to wait and watch for the pick-up car. Maybe I wasn't supposed to see the pick-up vehicle. Maybe he didn't want me to see his face. My eyes searched the thickets of mesquite and brambles. I couldn't see a car or a person in the dense foliage.

"Just drive away. I will find Juan Carlos and take him to Tucson," were the smuggler's directions.

And yet the whole thing just doesn't sit right with me. Where is this person who will pick up J.C.? Why didn't I see him parked nearby? Before driving away, I had seen a couple of cars parked at the side of the road. I drove past them slowly, peering into the cars' windows. One car had a woman in the driver's seat holding a cell phone to her ear. Another car had tinted glass; it was impossible to see the passengers. I spotted an Arizona Highway Patrol car behind me and immediately sped up. My heart sped up too. I turn onto the freeway and crank up the radio. Tom Petty is singing "Free Fallin.'" Yeah, right.

Several miles away I stop at a grocery store and pick up some milk and honey. I want to have honey in my cupboard if this ever happens again. When I return to this same location—the drop-off spot—I cruise slowly past, looking in the bushes for a sign of Juan Carlos. I see nothing. The dense thicket reminds me of the brambled bushes from the childhood tale of Br'er Rabbit and Br'er Fox. There is no way a person can navigate those bushes without tearing clothes to shreds, leaving bloody scratches on the skin. Feeling relief, I conclude that help has come for my friend and he's on his way to Nashville.

In fact, I feel like celebrating. There's a holiday party tonight at a neighboring ranch. I rush home, throw on my party clothes, try and talk Lester into coming with me (no luck), and drive to the festivities. I'm jubilant that I've made it through this experience without getting arrested. And J.C. is on his way to Tucson and then on to Nashville. I'm sure of it. Switching on the country-western station in the car, I hear Willie Nelson crooning "Crazy," and I sing along.

J.C. will thrive in his new life in the big city. He will create sushi and stir pots of boiling noodles, all with a red bandanna around his head. I see him sending money home to Guatemala. He's a good man, and I smile that I had a small part in this journey.

I want this image to be true so much that I can taste it.

Arriving at the party, I am high on the adventure. A potent margarita is thrust into my hand. I savor the salty rim of the glass and drink the tequila concoction far too fast. I'm dying to tell someone about the past forty-eight hours but decide to keep these things to myself. My secret life.

The tequila does its work. My mother used to call margaritas the drink with the velvet hammer. It softly takes over, clouding judgment and smoothing out the rough edges of life. It tastes like lemonade with a salty kick. I have another one.

Sitting on the stone hearth by a blazing fire, feeling the warmth of the flames and the tequila, I find myself pouring out the story of Juan Carlos to some people I barely know but intuitively trust. I've seen them at Samaritan meetings. Words spill out of my mouth and I say more than I should. They will understand, or at the very least won't turn me in to the cops. Feeling a flush in my cheeks and recognizing a few slurred words here and there, I tell it all. Most of it, anyway. They nod politely and look maybe a bit startled by my confession of harboring a lost and injured person.

"You saved a life today," one of them says. "Not many people can say that." Oh, how I needed to hear those words.

I am hungry to process this experience. I spot a priest across the room and impulsively walk over to him, unsure of how to proceed but desperately wanting to talk to someone wiser and more grounded than I am at this moment. I want someone to tell me how I could have handled this another way. What are the rules here? What should I do if this happens to me again? Has anyone written down a guidebook for this scenario? I want the priest to pray for Juan Carlos, and for me, too.

I am not Catholic and rarely attend church, but I need some spiritual direction here. I walk over to the padre and ask if I can see him sometime in the future to talk. The priest and I are friends, and he is curious about my query, so I give him a distilled version of the J.C. experience. There are people milling around us and I'm discreet with my words, but I need to talk. The tequila is still doing its job. I am tipsy, wired, and babbling nonstop and the priest and I agree to meet in the future. This party is not the place.

I immediately feel better. I have a plan.

Driving home that night, once again I slowly cruise by the drop-off point next to the railroad tracks. I peer into the bushes as I drive by, but it's dark and the rain is fogging up the car windows. It's impossible to see through the thicket of thorns and branches. I say a little prayer that J.C. was picked up by the stranger, the good-guy smuggler who will transport him to his sister. I hope this person has a generous heart. Perhaps Juan Carlos is well on his way northward to Nashville. Maybe he'll get there by Christmas.

There's a soft drizzle on the windshield, and I just want to arrive home and curl up by the fireplace. It is thirty-two degrees outside, and the drizzle is turning to sleet and ice. As I turn down the lane, I see that Lester has turned on the Christmas lights. The house looks cheery and welcoming and warm. I cannot imagine being outside on such a night.

THIRTEEN

So Near, So Far

Juan Carlos

MARGARITA DREW ME a map, and I look at the towns she has sketched along the way—Tubac, Green Valley, and finally Tucson. One of the points on the map is a border checkpoint, and I must be extremely careful when I am close to *la migra*. They all have guns. The rain continues to fall, and I follow a trail by the river, the Rio Santa Cruz.

There is an *iglesia* (church), a very old one, close to the river, and I hide in one of the ancient structures beside this holy place. Filling my water bottles from a garden hose at one of the adobe walls, I eat the small tin of sausages and drink deeply. A coyote is yipping in the distance, and I feel strangely at peace in this place. I pray to Jesus for strength and for safety. If only I could just stay here in this old mission building and work, perhaps as the gardener or a janitor. My eyes smart with tears. But I must stay strong. I must survive and find a way to get to Nashville.

I've come so far, and Margarita tells me it is three or four days to Tucson. Crouched in this shelter, I am getting cold, so I begin to walk again. If I make it to Tucson, I can call Alma and get a ride to Nashville. There are many Latinos in Tucson. Surely one of them will let me use a phone.

I walk until dawn and make a detour around the bright lights of what looks like the checkpoint. I count twelve green and white vans belonging to *la migra* and quietly creep through a *bosque* (forest) of trees and vines along the river far from the eyes of the agents. A few truckers go through the checkpoint at night, and I wonder if one of them would give me a ride.

I shake my head and put one foot in front of the other. Walking is the only way to freedom. I must keep moving. When it is daylight I will hide and rest; then the walking will continue after dark.

Walk. Walk. Walk.

The rain has stopped, and the sun warms me during the day. My jeans are wet and my socks are soaked. On a rock far from the highway I find a place to sit, where I take off my socks and jacket to dry them in the sun. I can hear the sounds of the trucks on the freeway, but see no one. For the moment I feel safe. Eating one of the chocolate bars and a banana stashed in my backpack, I feel drowsy and want to sleep. Soon I doze under a mesquite tree.

When I wake up it is afternoon, and I quickly look around to see if anyone has spotted me and my sleeping nest on the sunny rock. After gathering my socks and backpack together, I study the hand-drawn map smudged with damp, blurred pencil lines, and decide I will make it to Green Valley and maybe even to Tucson before tomorrow.

Shadows quickly gather in the December sky, and soon it is dusk. Maybe the people of Green Valley will help me get to Tucson. Maybe they will let me use their phone to call Alma.

Maybe. Maybe. Maybe.

My only reality is putting one foot in front of the other. I brush my dreams aside and begin walking.

The days and nights are constant walking, resting, walking, resting. I try to walk for three hours and rest for three hours. On the third day I see the lights of Tucson. Or I think it is Tucson. My back muscles are on fire; my feet have blisters that have broken and now are replaced by new blisters. I look for a church where I might feel safe, but see nothing. Only cars and stores and the smell of frying food at the drive-ins. The stench of my body overwhelms me, and I have a rash under my arms and between my legs. I am sweating one moment and wracked with shivers the next.

Falling to my knees in an arroyo, I make a decision. I cannot walk one more step. I will turn myself in to *la migra* and plead for mercy. I will tell them of my life in Guatemala and the fact that guns have been pointed at my head. The American government will help me find a place to live in safety. My wife and children can join me. I will work hard and learn to love my new country. I cannot hide anymore.

Tears are streaming down my cheeks and I am embarrassed to feel these emotions. Wiping them away with the back of my hands, I look for *la migra* and the green and white cars that carry the captured migrants. It is five o'clock in the afternoon, and I do not see one Border Patrol van. I am walking along a busy highway and there is no one who stops. I desperately wave at the cars passing by. No one slows down.

I start to laugh. Hiding in the desert for three days, I had shielded myself like a rabbit from the hawk that stalks its prey, using bushes and rocks as camouflage. Now I am out in the open, begging for capture, and there is no *la migra*. God is mocking me. First I make a croaking, laughing sound that does not sound like me. Then I fall to my knees and pound the dirt.

Finally I see a car with red lights flashing and wave at it, the *policia*. The officer speaks Spanish and asks me for my identification.

"I am Juan Carlos, and I have walked to this place from Guatemala," I tell him.

He has a kind face and his skin is brown like mine. "Guatemala is a long way from home, *amigo*."

He smiles at me, opens the back door of his vehicle, and tells me to get in. He gives me water and a packet of *galletas* (cookies).

"Feliz Navidad," he says.

Jesucristo! It is Christmas Day! I bow my head in the back seat of the police car and begin to sob. Then I rip open the packet of cookies and devour all of them. I drink the bottle of water in two long swallows.

As I taste the sweetness of the cookies, I am overcome with gratitude for this simple moment in my life. The cookies and water remind me of communion in my church back home. They are Oreos, the body of Christ. The water is the blood. It is a sign. My Savior will see me through this. I am on my knees in the back of the police car, promising God that I will change my ways and repent my sins.

I pray that this *americano* police officer will treat me with respect. To be standing under a hot shower is my fantasy for the entire ride to the police station.

Later that night I am taken to another city and another cell for Latinos who have been caught in *los Estados Unidos* without their papers. The city is called Florence, and my clothes and backpack are taken from me. I do not know what will happen and I do not care. I stand under a hot shower for as long as the guard will allow, and I smile in gratitude.

FOURTEEN

Awakening

Margarita

I WAIT SEVEN days and call Alma in Nashville. It is December 30. Hoping that J.C. is safe with this family, I'm anxious to hear about his journey.

All week I've envisioned J.C. traveling in a warm, comfortable car to Nashville, stopping along the way for burgers, tacos, and lots of Cokes. I've seen him sitting in Denny's all-night cafés drinking black coffee and looking at maps while his driver buys him the Grand Slam breakfast. Alma and her husband greet him, and he delights in the Christmas tree, the children, the merriment. He's safe, warm, and out of danger.

Alma douses me with reality.

"He was captured by the *policia* and is in jail. They put him in jail on Christmas Day."

Alma doesn't know the name of the town or the state. Nor does she have any telephone number or other contact information.

"Was the driver also captured and put in prison?" I ask, stunned by this news.

Alma tells me a story I have heard so many times from migrants at *el comedor*, the aid station in Nogales. The smuggler demands the money and never delivers the service. The family was duped by a scam artist.

"Please slow down, Alma. Please tell me this news again," I plead, struggling to take in this shocking development.

Jaime gets on the phone and tells me the rest of the story.

"We wired the driver the money, but he never met Juan Carlos at the freeway exit. He just took the money from the Western Union office and disappeared. He was my friend. He is no one's friend now."

My breath comes in short gasps, and my stomach feels like it's full of cold stones. On my drive-by cruises at the drop-off point seven days ago, Juan Carlos was probably crouching in one of those bushes. Maybe he even recognized my car. And I kept right on going.

Overwhelmed by guilt and sadness, I stare into space. Jaime keeps talking, but I hear nothing. Though Juan Carlos and I didn't know each other very well, I'm feeling responsible. I dropped him off in the middle of winter on one of the coldest and most miserable nights of the year. My gut instincts were correct: There was something fishy about this whole operation. There was no family friend (aka smuggler) to transport J.C.

Sitting in my cozy home with a fire flickering in the corner fireplace, beans bubbling on the stove, wrapped in the safety and warmth of my life, I cannot believe that Juan Carlos is now enmeshed in the hell-hole of our criminal justice system. Picked up on Christmas Day.

I realize that I don't know how to spell Juan Carlos's full name and am chagrined at the lack of information I have about him.

"What is Juan Carlos's full name? What is his wife's name? Where exactly does he live in Guatemala?"

I ask Jaime for basic information about this man, who entered our lives more dead than alive. I know next to nothing. Jaime carefully spells out Juan Carlos's full name, and I strain to understand the spelling and get it right.

I decide to track him down. Maybe I'll drive to wherever he's being incarcerated and see if there's anything I can do to help him. Maybe he needs some money. I wonder if he knows his rights. What are his rights? Does he have any rights?

When I go online and search for information about how to locate an undocumented person in the Arizona prison system, it's a labyrinth of confusion. There are many prisons and detention centers. Is he in Arizona? Where did they take him?

I begin calling the list of private prisons and federal facilities. Wading through the automated voice systems to get to a real person is daunting in itself. I'm usually transferred to someone's voice mail, and my message is lost in the ethers. I leave six messages at six facilities. No one calls me back.

This goes on for days. Finally I reach a sympathetic person in Florence who says he can help me.

"You need an A-number," he tells me curtly, but with a hint of human connection.

"The what?"

"You need to get the Alien Registration Number, and then we can locate your friend."

"But how do I get the A-number if I don't know where he is in your prison system?" I slowly spell out Juan Carlos's full name, his country of origin, and the day he was picked up by the police. The agent in Florence is dismissive of this information.

"Well, there are a lot of people here, ma'am, and we go by the A-numbers. You need to find out what his number is." He hangs up on me.

I call Alma in Nashville. She doesn't know what I'm talking about and has no knowledge of an A-number. She has not spoken to her brother since the police picked him up on Christmas Day. Alma sounds like she's been crying for days.

"Please find my baby brother," she says.

Calling back the one phone number where I found a real person, and not just the automated voice, I get a string of bureaucratic, disinterested receptionists who are clearly annoyed that I don't have the sacred A-number.

Days pass. I call in the morning, I call in the evening. No one wants to help me.

Finally, after a week of pestering several different men on the other end of the phone line, I miraculously get the same person who told me about the A-number. I recognize his Texan accent, which has a smidgen of humanity in it. In my nicest, most submissive voice, I basically beg this guy to help me out. I tell him I have Juan Carlos's full name and country of birth.

"Please, can you look through your list of names and tell me if he is in your prison?"

It's a Sunday night and I sense that the guy has a little time to kill. I can hear the rustle of papers, the clanging of metal doors, and echoing voices in the background. Some country-western music is playing on a radio—Waylon Jennings belting out one of his tunes about wild women and good whiskey. The fellow on the phone has good taste in country music, so I figure there must be some humanity present in this particular prison office. If you like Waylon Jennings, you can't be all bad.

"So what is your relationship to this person?" The sympathetic phone person is all business—blunt, but willing to hang in there with me. "Why do you want to contact him?"

"He's a friend, and I just found out that he's been detained somewhere in your detention prison system."

"Are you family?"

I hesitate. And then I begin to spin a tale.

"The family lives in Nashville, too far to travel. I live in Arizona and want to visit this person and be in contact with the family. I am an unofficial member of this family."

Continuing to babble on and embellish the story, I talk about a long friendship with his family in Guatemala. Basically, I lie and act like I've known this fellow for years.

"So what is your name? Where do you live?"

I'm stopped cold by this question but give out my personal contact information like I trust him and everyone in charge of the prison. I have no idea what the repercussions will be. I take the plunge.

"Just a minute. I'll see if I can find anything."

The phone contact person scans through a data-base, and I'm on "hold" for several minutes. I fear I've lost the one real-time voice in this universe of prisons and bureaucracy. Tempted to end this wild goose chase to nowhere, I almost hang up. But then he returns and tells me he found Juan Carlos's name on the list of asylum seekers. Bingo! He is in a detention center in Florence, and I get the all-important A-number. I'm ready to tattoo this number on my forehead.

I am so grateful for this phone receptionist, this fellow who took the time to search through his lists. I gush out my thank-you's like I'm a prisoner myself—a prisoner to a rigid bureaucratic system of rules and protocols.

Like a fool, I ask the receptionist if he likes his job. "It's okay, but I want to get out of Florence and find something in Tucson," he says. I chatter on about the opportunities in Tucson, of which I know next to nothing. I'm like a starving puppy hungry for scraps, and this fellow has thrown me a delicious morsel, the A-number. And I add that I love Waylon Jennings and hope he has a pleasant evening.

⸻ • ⸻

I SCHEDULE A visit with Juan Carlos at the prison site in early January. Setting up a meeting at the detention center is not an easy task. I'm transferred to another line, put on hold interminably, but by the grace of God am not disconnected.

The receptionist will let J.C. know that I'm coming the second week of January. Writing a note to Juan Carlos, I let him know when I'm coming and give him my telephone number. We will meet at high noon.

My letter is returned a day before our meeting. I neglected to put the all-important A-number on the envelope. J.C. doesn't know I'm making the three-hour trip to Florence.

Feeling anxious about this encounter, I obsess about all the things that have gone wrong. I left J.C. in a gnarly thicket of brambles in the dead of winter without a cell phone and without making sure his driver was there to pick him up. He wanders alone for three days along a river bed, surrounded by State Police, Border Patrol agents, hostile Americans, and snarling dogs. Hiding in mesquite thickets and cow pastures, he walks miles with minimal supplies or warm clothes. On Christmas Day he makes it to a city and turns himself over to the American authorities.

Why in hell would he want to see me?

Feelings of incompetence in offering real substantial help to J.C. engulf me. He could have died. The least I can do now is try to get him some legal help.

My knowledge of how to assist him while he is in the detention center is zilch.

I call a lawyer friend, and he recommends that I call the Florence Project, which is a pro bono group of law students and attorneys. They visit detainees at the detention center and provide information and advice. Speaking Spanish, they're able to communicate the detailed and complicated instructions clearly to the thousands who are incarcerated for the crime of crossing our borders without the necessary papers.

In early January I travel to Florence as planned and then spend another hour or more driving up and down unmarked entry roads, trying to find the building where detainees are locked up. Initially, all I can see are block-shaped buildings hiding behind the world's largest collection of razor wire. Florence has nine ways to lock you up—in facilities run by county, state, federal and private for-profit corporations. Both sides of the highway are blanketed with one-story buildings, razor wire and towers. I have no idea which one houses my migrant friend from Guatemala.

After turning in to one of the prison complexes, a federal facility, I hunt for the office. In the parking lot I walk around a couple of anonymous looking buildings until I see someone come out of an unmarked door. I figure this must be the entrance and walk into the office asking where I might find my friend, Juan Carlos. I'm met with a puzzled stare, and a uniformed man brusquely asks me how I got into this office.

"I parked my car in your lot and I walked through this door."

"You aren't allowed in here. How did you get past the guards? You aren't allowed in here!" He is barking at me.

I'm flustered and feel like I've unwittingly trespassed into forbidden territory. Everyone in the office is looking at me like I'm some sort of threat to their smooth-running operation. An unwelcome guest.

"I need some direction here," I explain. "Where are the detainees from Central America?"

"Well, they're not here. Try across the street, about a mile up the road. You're looking for the Central Arizona Detention Center. This is the Arizona Federal Prison."

A guard escorts me to my car and tells me that the public isn't allowed in this parking lot. I am intimidated by his inhospitable demeanor and ask where the "Keep Out" signs are. Did I miss something when I drove in?

He shrugs and watches me climb into my vehicle and drive away. I hate this place already, and haven't even found the building that houses the undocumented migrants. I'm tempted to bail on the whole idea but decide to persevere. It feels like one of those Escher paintings with all the stair-steps leading to nowhere. I'm caught in a painting.

I drive up the road and I stop at another complex of buildings. There are no signs to direct me to the Central Arizona Detention Center. A fellow in a uniform stands in an enclosed cubicle in front of a high barricade fence with more circles of concertina wire on top.

"Is this the Central Arizona Detention Center? I don't see any sign, and need to find the right building."

"Yep. You're in the right place," the officer in the cubicle replies.

"How come there are no signs?" I ask.

Mr. Prison Officer shrugs. No answer.

"I have an appointment with Juan Carlos and here is his A-number." I have my ducks in a row and am feeling smug.

"So what's your relationship to this person?" he asks as he shuffles through a list of inmates and numbers. I wonder why this is any business of the officer in the cubicle. Do you have to be blood-related to visit a prisoner?

"I'm a friend of the family. They live too far away to visit."

After scanning a list of names, the agent tells me that Juan Carlos has a medical appointment at noon but I can come back at one. I ask if J.C. is sick, and the agent shrugs again.

"I have no idea. You'll have to ask the guard."

So I sit outside the prison on metal benches bolted around picnic tables. Several other families are gathered here. They all look Latino, and the children play with sticks and pebbles, knocking the stones around in the dirt of the landscaped cactus garden. The mood feels upbeat, with the soft cadence of Spanish surrounding me in this group of mostly women and children. There is one adult male, smoking a cigarette a few feet away.

The group looks at me curiously, as I am the only *gringa* in the crowd. It's a sparkling January day in Arizona, and the sun radiates a blinding brilliance off the concrete walkways and buildings as it sits low in the winter sky. I wish I could grab a stick and play with the children and capture some of their innocence and joy in this courtyard. The adults are silent; the children shriek when they spot a lizard and chase it under a rock. The kids are all scrubbed and neatly dressed.

"Don't get dirty before you see your Papá," their mother tells them.

Soon the guard calls out my name and tells me Juan Carlos is available for a visitation. But first I must leave my purse, jewelry, watch, pen, paper, keys and cell phone in a locker. A female agent pats me down, checking for weapons and drugs.

"Is it okay if I take my Spanish-English dictionary so I can communicate better? My Spanish isn't that great."

"Absolutely not," the agent curtly replies. She is Mexican-American and speaks fluent Spanish as well as English. I look at her incredulously.

"You can't exchange any written communication or bring any items in with you," she says flatly.

"But I don't understand? I'm not going to give my friend this dictionary. I just want to communicate with him."

The agent is unyielding. "Put the dictionary in the locker with all of your other stuff."

There is no further discussion. She gives me a locker key which I hang around my neck on a leather cord.

I leave my personal items behind, and as I follow the agent through the wire fence and locked gates, I realize I have no identification on me at all. I feel vulnerable, anxious, and paranoid. My mind turns to irrational scenarios. What if I'm kidnapped in this maze of buildings and no one believes me when I tell them my name? I could get locked away in one of the back buildings and never be found. Basically, I don't trust these people who are leading me around this colorless maze of sidewalks and fences. And they don't like me very much either.

Blinded by the sunlight on the beige and white buildings, I decide that this is the most boring and nondescript set of buildings I've ever seen. There is absolutely no color anywhere—no grass, flowers, or visual contrast to the blandness of these cell blocks. The gravel in the yard reflects the glare from the winter sun and temporarily renders me sightless. I shade my eyes with my right hand and submissively follow the officious agent through a maze of sidewalks and doorways. We don't speak during our walk through the prison grounds. Every building looks the same. I see no one wandering outside the fences or inside the barricades.

We reach yet another set of locked gates and enter a security zone where I'm asked to remove my shoes, and pass through an X-ray machine. When the alarm goes off, I must step aside and am patted down again. As I pass through the X-ray machine a second time, the guard tells me that the alarm on the machine is often activated for no discernible reason. An agent asks me where I live and why I'm visiting. I tell him I'm a friend of the family, and am concerned about the welfare of the man from Guatemala. He looks at me curiously, like he doesn't believe me.

I see several vending machines in the waiting area and am told I can purchase a voucher for an inmate if I wish, so he can get chips, candy, cigarettes.

"But my purse with my money is locked up in a locker out by the entrance to this place."

The agent shrugs as if this is my problem and not his. Which is correct. I make a mental note to return to this room with the vending machines carrying some money. J.C. should have some vouchers for snack foods and treats.

I don't find the prison guards rude or disrespectful; however, they are nonplussed and disinterested in my questions. Helping me is not in their job description—customer service is nonexistent—and before long they become impatient with me. They seem annoyed that I don't know the ropes. The guards definitely have the upper hand here, and I'm an incompetent intruder in their well-regulated, monitored work life. I feel as if this is my first day at school. I'm a slow learner.

The guard leads me through two more locked gates until we come to the visiting area, a large room with bolted-down tables and chairs. Sitting at one of the tables is Juan Carlos in navy blue prison garb— draw string pants and a cotton V-neck pullover shirt. The clothes look like surgical scrubs. His eyes light up, eager and surprised to see me, and he gives me a huge smile. Actually, he looks pretty good. He's gained some weight, and his black hair is cropped short.

Checking in at the guard station, I ask for a pen or pencil to write down information that would be helpful to J.C..

"No, ma'am! You are not allowed to write anything down while visiting." The guard looks at me like I was asking for the moon.

As I walk over to J.C., we both look at the guards and cameras, scoping out the situation. Reaching across the table, he squeezes my hands and begins a litany of "thank you's" and "God bless you's." I'm his first visitor, and he has been here three weeks. We're both self-conscious about this visit, not quite knowing what is appropriate. I want to give him a hug but am unsure of prison decorum. Without my Spanish-English dictionary, the conversation is a struggle for both of us.

There is a Mexican family at the next table visiting their loved one, and a teenage girl is smiling at my halting efforts with the Spanish verbs and nouns. I ask the girl to help with the translation.

The young teen is about fifteen, with beautiful, lustrous black hair to her waist, and is happy to oblige. She leans across the aisle to help me with my primitive Spanish. She and J.C. begin an animated conversation in Spanish and she quickly translates for me, telling me about his walk to Tucson and turning himself in to the authorities after three days. I

learn that he spent some time in the federal prison before being transferred to this detention center. Asking for asylum, he needs legal counsel.

Suddenly, three guards surround our table. "No cross-talking with
other inmates," one of them bellows. The young teen looks startled, and
I stand up, explaining that she was merely helping me translate because
I wasn't allowed to carry my Spanish-English dictionary into this room.

"Absolutely no talking with others in this room. No exceptions!"

"Please don't shout at us," I sputter. "I asked this girl for help. This
is my fault."

The teenager, J.C., and I are scolded like school-children speaking
out of turn. Except these guys are armed, menacing, and act like we
have committed a cardinal sin—the sin of communication. We all bow
our heads apologetically, and the teen returns to her own table with
her family. Juan Carlos looks shaken and stares at me. His position is
far more vulnerable than mine.

I'm both intimidated and angered by the reprimand. Juan Carlos
and I sit quietly for some moments, our hands folded meekly. I try to
measure what would be the best thing to do: assert myself and raise a
little hell about being scolded like a naughty child, or just sit here pas-
sively and allow the moment to pass.

I walk across the room to the enclosed guard station and ask if they
could help me find a lawyer for my friend from Guatemala. Four uniformed men and a woman stare back at me blankly as if they have never
been asked such a question.

One guard finally answers. "There is an office called the Florence
Project, and they have lawyers that can help you." He gives me eye
contact and acts like he wants to help me.

I grab on to this small indication of humanity and tread carefully
with my words and actions.

"Could you please write down an address or phone number for me?" No one moves in the guard station. "I've heard about this project, but don't know where their office located."

"As you know, I'm not allowed to have a pencil or paper in here." A couple of the guards roll their eyes and turn away from me like I'm the dumbest thing in the room. And I probably am.

One guard jots down some information for me on a sticky note. The others look at him like he's breaking the rules, stepping out of the box.

"I'll give it to you after you're through with your visit." The guard is curt, his affect flat. He is uncomfortable sharing information with me and is walking a narrow line between conforming to the prison guard norms, and helping me out. I am grateful for his risk-taking.

One guard shakes his head. In disapproval? In exasperation with my request? I really don't know.

"You know, we call Juan Carlos the 'Christmas migrant,' because we picked him up on Christmas Day," he says with a small grin.

"We nicknamed him J.C.," another guard adds. "Probably didn't walk here from Bethlehem, though."

Everyone laughs at the Bethlehem joke. For a brief moment there is connection and friendliness with the guards, and they smile at me. I relax and try to engage them, realizing I can get some help if I just say the right words, push the right buttons, avoid raising hackles. I begin to feel like maybe these guys will cut me some slack and help me out after all.

I express my appreciation for this information and assistance, adding that I drove three hours to get to Florence and I want to help my friend.

"Your rules about no books, no pencils, no paper make it very difficult to help this person who is fleeing for his life."

"We have our code of conduct and our rules," one says. "This isn't a country club." They're hard as nails.

"But I thought when you request asylum, the country where you wish to resettle had a more welcoming process in place. Not a prison." I looked to the guards for an answer.

"Where did you hear that?" one of the guards says and chuckles.

"There are strict requirements, and not many migrants ever get asylum," another adds. "Are you family? He needs to have family in the U.S. to even consider getting asylum."

"So how do you know this man from Guatemala?"

I'm immediately on guard. Are they going to forbid my visitation because I'm not family? Again I spin a story about family friends and ties in Guatemala. J.C. watches me with a perplexed expression as I fabricate a tale for the guard. I look back at J.C., who is quietly observing this scene from his cold, hard institutional bench. In this colorless room, I realize I have a lot to learn about asylum and how my country handles refugees fleeing violence. There is no welcome mat, to be sure.

After returning to the prison table and my conversation with J.C., I soon run out of words to say. Not wanting me to leave, he struggles to tell me about his life in this prison.

"The food is better than the first place I was taken." He pats his stomach as if he is turning into an *hombre gordo* (fat man). We both laugh at the absurdity of this notion.

He's made some friends in his cell block, and they're teaching him English. There are never any books or magazines in the library. He is incredibly bored and alone and afraid.

"I'll be back," I tell him. "I'll try and find a lawyer who can explain your options."

We say our good-byes, and the guard gives me the address for the Florence Project.

"It's right across the street in a little white house. You can't miss it," he tells me.

After leaving the prison complex, I stop by the Florence Project. The place is locked up and no one answers my knocks on the door. I jot down the phone number that's taped to the door and plan to call the office before my next trip to this sad little town.

FIFTEEN

Detention

Margarita

If I had one wish, it would be for fluency in Spanish. I'm hopeless, and my aging brain is like a sieve, with those reflexive verbs and past tenses disappearing down the drain. Nevertheless, I stumble along, swallowing my pride when I use the wrong vocabulary, and do my best to connect with my Latino friends.

One of my Samaritan colleagues is a retired Spanish teacher from Michigan who spends her winters in Green Valley, Arizona, with her husband. I approach her at a Samaritan meeting and ask if she would drive to Florence with me and be my translator during my next visit. She agrees, and in two weeks Marylyn and I are on a roadie trip to the Florence prison to see Juan Carlos. I've also made contact with the Florence Project and plan to stop in there as well.

In February, Marylyn and I drive to Florence for my second visit with Juan Carlos, and this trip goes much better. The communication is vastly improved with Marylyn's help, and Juan Carlos tells us that someone official, perhaps an attorney, has come to visit him and told him of his rights as a person seeking asylum.

Juan Carlos speaks directly to Marylyn in rapid-fire Spanish but maintains eye contact with me. His voice cracking with emotion, he wipes away tears as he speaks of his nights in the snowy mountains of the desert. He tells us he saw "twenty-five *puercos*," the marauding *javelinas* that were looking for food during the December weeks of frigid temperatures.

"I would wake up in the night and the pigs were surrounding me. Throwing rocks scared them a little bit, but they would come back."

His face, taut with the trauma of haunting memories, is the face of fear. He recalls his nights of terror in the desert and tells us stories that still bring tears to his eyes. Feeling like I'm not doing enough for this man, I wish I knew more about the law and chastise myself for the hundredth time about my lack of Spanish proficiency.

But here we are, the three of us, doing our best to connect with each other. Mentally I'm making a list: Find a lawyer for Juan Carlos, leave him some money for incidentals and phone calls at the prison, and be an advocate for him when his hearing is scheduled.

Stopping at the Florence Project, I speak with one of the pro bono attorneys who are volunteering on behalf of migrants seeking asylum. He is attentive and interested and promises to talk with Juan Carlos within the week. His message is both encouraging and discouraging. Because J.C. has one of the most dangerous jobs in Guatemala—driving a bus—his reports of extortion and deadly threats will be taken seriously. This is the good news.

However, J.C. has already entered the United States illegally. Three times, in fact. He was caught once, and there are records of his detention in McAllen, Texas. He turned himself in on his last illegal entry six weeks ago. His previous deportation (in 2011) could exclude him from resettlement in the U.S. Plus, his family in Nashville is undocumented. J.C. has no one to sponsor him once he's resettled. Family members must be citizens or legal immigrants with papers in order to sponsor an asylum seeker. The attorney tells me it will be at least six months before J.C. has a hearing, and then another twelve to eighteen months before a final decision will be rendered.

Bottom line: The odds are slim that he will be granted asylum. But not hopeless. The Florence Project attorney tells me that a lot depends on the judge assigned to the case and on the documentation that J.C. collects to prove the dangers he faces in Guatemala if he returns.

I make a mental note to call Alma and ask her and the family to write a letter regarding the dangers her brother faced as a bus driver in Guatemala. We must obtain documentation proving there were assaults and extortion on J.C.

After our meeting with the attorney, Marylyn and I walk back to the prison, this time with my debit card stuffed in my jeans pocket, and I arrange for some cash vouchers for Juan Carlos. Again, the process is confusing, and I'm shuffled around from one office to another by brusque agents who would rather be staring at their computer screens or chatting it up with their colleagues. I'm definitely interrupting their day with my ineptness. I watch as an agent plays video solitaire on his computer.

Eventually we get the job done. I leave some money for vouchers so Juan Carlos can buy some snack food from the vending machine. Privately I wonder if he will ever get the vouchers.

Driving back home that night with Marylyn, I feel like I've fallen down a rabbit hole. The world of the Florence prison runs on a different set of rules, and I'm clueless about negotiating my way through the endless locked doors. The agents are either obnoxious or inappropriately flirtatious. Often they're both. Maybe my attempts to engage with the prison guards were misinterpreted. Who knows?

Arriving home, I pour myself a glass of wine and stare out the window at the desert sunset. I wonder how this is all going to play out.

During the next few months, Juan Carlos calls me (collect) several times from the prison. We talk about his days in lock-up, and he sounds discouraged. A few times I speak with a fellow Latino inmate whom Juan Carlos has asked to talk with me. He's proficient in English, and he tells me that J.C. is quite depressed. I make two more trips to the Florence prison to see him and do my best to bolster his spirits. Privately I worry about his suicide potential. J.C. has no one outside the prison except me who has some potential for helping him. And I'm pretty useless.

I write a letter to the prison officials:

February 5, 2014

To Whom It May Concern:
Re: Juan Carlos xxxxxx
Central Arizona Detention Center
Florence, AZ. 85232
    I am a friend of Juan Carlos and his family in Nashville, Tennessee. Juan is seeking asylum in the United States and is fleeing the violence of his home in Guatemala. He has experienced death threats and guns pointed to his head as a bus driver in Guatemala. He cannot return without facing possible torture and death.
    I met Juan Carlos in a shelter in Nogales, Sonora, Mexico, and have great respect for his work ethic and strength of character. If I can be any help in obtaining asylum for this man, I am willing to do so.
    Thank you for considering his request for asylum in the United States. His family in Tennessee is willing to assist him in any way possible.
    Because this case means a long period of incarceration at the Detention Center, I request that Juan Carlos be transferred to a

facility in Tennessee where he has access to his family of origin.
Thank you for your consideration and humanitarian action
in the case of Juan Carlos xxxxxx.

Sincerely,
Margaret Bowden

In the letter I have lied about knowing J.C.'s family in Nashville and about meeting him at the *comedor*, the aid station in Nogales. To tell the truth about Juan Carlos's odyssey in the desert and his time in our home doesn't make any sense. I would be admitting to harboring a fugitive.

I receive no response to my letter.

March comes, and I decide to spend Easter in Mexico, something I've wanted to do for many years. I will live with the people of Mexico and work on my Spanish.

I travel to Alamos, a colonial city in Sonora, and rent a house for a month. My plan is to study Spanish and experience what life is like for an American living in this lovely city of cobblestones and arches. Before leaving on this trip, I tell Juan Carlos of my plan and my desire to speak Spanish with more fluency.

"We can have real conversations when I return in late April," I explain. He looks at me in a manner that immediately distances himself from me. I have dropped a bomb. He asks me to repeat what I've just said about my plans to live in Alamos for a month. He can't believe I'm disappearing for a month—maybe more.

I feel like I'm deserting him, and once again realize that I'm the only lifeline he has. Representing hope and possibilities, I brought my small gifts of money and American support each time I drove to the prison.

"Don't give up," I tell him.

He gives me a wan smile and nods.

"Practice your English. Go to the library. Read the American newspapers." He shrugs and tells me the library is empty. The books are either checked out or they've disappeared. He looks close to tears. He doesn't look at me.

I try to connect him with attorneys and legal aides who can explain his options. Of course, what I learn from my attorney friends is that there really are no options for Juan Carlos. Unless the immigration policies of my country change, a person with a record of repeated illegal entry has an extremely slim chance of achieving asylum.

I feel like I'm doing nothing, really. Our meetings at the detention center leave me depressed and disheartened. I drive home in a funk. I actually begin to dread his phone calls because I don't know what to tell him. I'm always the first to end our phone conversations. I simply run out of steam and vocabulary.

"Hang in there. You are strong. You will get through this," is my mantra. I hate giving out such empty platitudes. It reminds me of my experiences as a nurse, dishing out pain pills to critically ill patients when I knew the pills would barely make a dent in their suffering.

And I'm learning something about myself. Going the extra mile with this one soul has been fraught with complications and inconsistencies. I'm exhausted, stressed, and ill-equipped to handle his needs. I wish he had stumbled onto another patio last December and connected with a savvy lawyer or a more sophisticated network of people who knew how to get this man to Nashville. When I took on this relationship, I thought I had the knowledge and guts to truly make a difference. I was wrong.

I feel like shit. And that's an understatement.

════▶ • ◀════

April 2014

A THICK ENVELOPE is waiting for me at the ranch after my month-long hiatus in Alamos. Inside is a photo of Juan Carlos's wife and two young children, his family. The little boy looks to be about five years old, and is dressed up in a blue plaid shirt and clean jeans. He has a rakish, toothy grin on his face, and his arms are around his mother's neck. The child is standing on a rock border fence hugging his mother. I'm sure the person behind the camera has told the group to "smile."

His daughter, about age three, is dressed in a party frock. She has neatly combed hair and a pensive half-smile. The woman, his wife, wears a brightly printed blouse and a light blue plaid skirt. She has a round face and a warm gaze as she looks into the camera. Her expression is engaging, but not happy. She does not smile. She looks tired and resigned. The three cling to each other. The photo looks like it was taken in a city with manicured shrubs and trees.

On the back of the photo is printed in pencil: "This is a souvenir for Margarita Peg Bowden. It is my family that lives in Guatemala. Take care of this special remembrance."

There is a letter inside the envelope, written in careful cursive penciled on a yellow legal pad.

Florence, Arizona
April 20, 2014

Margarita,

I hope this letter finds you well. Greetings to you and yours in the name of Jesus Christ our Savior. I am very grateful to you for helping me. I will always carry thoughts of you in my heart and will always remember you in my prayers to God for your help when I was almost dying in the desert. Thank you for your help and the food you gave me.

Tomorrow, Monday, I will return to Guatemala and I'll never forget this contact with you. This is my number in Guatemala: 011 xxx-xxxxxxx for you to communicate with me.

Here are the letters that were sent to me from Guatemala telling why I was coming here to the U.S. The reason for my return was that my family is having a hard time and is in great need.

That is why I had to return. My incarceration has been very difficult and my children have gotten sick. Thank you, thank you, a thousand thank you's; may God grant you a long life.

I wanted to talk with your husband at some time, to greet him, but unfortunately I couldn't because I couldn't speak much English. But greet him on my behalf, please.

Immigration has told me that my case would last a year, and here inside [prison] I have to fight it. And there is more. But they gave me some papers that say there are possibilities that I could return legally to the United States. They [also] gave me this number to call there:

(202) xxx-xxxx

Office of the Public Advocate, Enforcement and Removal Operations

U.S. Immigration and Customs Enforcement

500 12th Street SW

Washington, DC 20536

EROPublicAdvocate@ice.dhs.gov

As soon as I return, I'll look for work or change the place I was living.

Thank you for everything and may God bless you for everything. I would like to ask you a favor: I have two children. If you could help me pay for their schooling I'll show you my gratitude when I return and start again. Again, take care and may God give you a long life.

Juan Carlos

Also contained in the manila envelope are three letters from employers in Guatemala affirming the dangerous conditions that J.C. encountered as he drove a bus through the streets of Guatemala City and Xela. After placing all these documents in a file folder, I sit at my desk and close my eyes.

Why is helping this man so incredibly difficult?

SIXTEEN

Back to Square One

AUTUMN 2014
Margarita

SETTLING BACK INTO the rhythms of life on our ranch, I'm eager to practice my fragile gains in conversational Spanish with Juan Carlos. But of course he is gone, back to Guatemala. I ponder the content of his letter to me and feel guilty about not knowing how to do more for him legally, financially, politically. The whole thing is just wrong. J.C. is back where he started, in a country that's unpredictable, volatile, corrupt, and poverty-stricken.

If I dig deep enough inside, I am also relieved. I no longer have to figure all of this out. Living in a country where there are no pathways for people like J.C., I have spent a lot of hours and miles spinning my wheels. I don't have to do that anymore. Nestling back in my own comfortable cocoon, I can return to my life of security. No more long drives to the Florence prison and no confusing conversations with lawyers. It is done.

But I think about Juan Carlos a lot.

I try to call him twice with the phone number he left me. There is a long robotic message in Spanish and a lot of crackling during the transmission. No one answers.

Maybe he's driving that bus in Guatemala City with a gun pointed to his head. Maybe he never made it home and is somewhere in Central America planting coffee beans and living in a shack, sending money home to his wife and children.

I replay the past months in my mind, wondering what I could have done differently. When I spoke to some lawyer friends, they didn't have a lot of advice to offer. They shrugged and said that his downfall was crossing illegally so many times and getting caught.

On my cell phone I type in the numbers of some lawyers at the Florence Project, plus a Tucson church that offers sanctuary. Somehow taking these steps helps in an odd way that makes absolutely no sense. I can call people who have already told me they can do nothing.

In the evenings at home I look out over the desert and say a silent prayer that no one will come knocking at our door needing help. I am a failure at this helping game.

———— • ————

So, fleeing a country where he has a good chance of getting shot, or his family could starve, or he could be extorted every week by renegade gangs—these are not reasons enough to obtain help and sanctuary from the richest country in the world. J.C. is back in Guatemala to face his fate.

When does an asylum seeker become a refugee? What does it take?

The business of asylum is a complex web of legal gobbledygook. If you've crossed illegally into the United States before and have been deported, you're subject to a process called "reinstatement of removal." Juan Carlos crossed into the U.S. illegally three times; he was caught once, and turned himself in once, landing in a detention center. After the one successful crossing, he lived in Nashville for several years, working at a restaurant.

Those in reinstatement of removal proceedings who fear returning to their country are afforded a "reasonable fear" interview with an asylum officer. Juan Carlos had an interview with a U.S Citizenship and Immigration Services (USCIS) officer regarding his fear of persecution and torture should he return to his home and job in Guatemala. The officer determined that J.C. was eligible for a deferral of removal. In other words, he would not be immediately deported but instead could stay at the detention center until his immigration hearing was scheduled. He was told he would have to wait twelve to eighteen months for a hearing.

In 2016, the U.S. immigration court and asylum systems were backlogged with more than 620,000 pending removal and asylum cases. Wait times of up to six years for asylum seekers were not uncommon.

And there is a cryptic line in his letter to me about his time in the Florence detention center. When expressing how difficult it was to remain inside the prison, he wrote, *"And there is more."* He never clarified what things he faced each day. I never found out what the "more" entailed. Was there physical abuse? Sexual abuse? For sure, there was racism and power and manipulation and verbal abuse. I witnessed some of this myself.

Our country has built a network of detention centers where asylum seekers and immigration violators are locked up and await their hearings, their interviews, their due process. These detainees are not criminals or convicts serving sentences. They are locked up because the U.S. government wants to make sure they show up in immigration court. Detainees are punished far beyond the scale of their offense. Their only offense is fleeing for their lives. This kind of mass incarceration shatters families, traumatizes children, and costs the taxpayers billions of dollars.

The private prison system in the United States is a profitable business. The Department of Homeland Security keeps thirty-four thousand beds occupied every day, no matter the need. Imprisoning people who are fleeing the violence of their home country is inhumane.

That's the only way I can slice it.

SEVENTEEN

─── • ───

A Real Tortilla

Juan Carlos

FLYING IN A jet high above the desert, the place where I almost died, I think about Maria and my children. I feel shame. Tears sting my eyes and I do my best to blink them away. Will little Lupita know me? Is the family angry that I wasted our money trying to get to Nashville and steady work? Do they know I'm coming home? Maybe I should have stayed and tried for asylum. Maybe Margarita could have helped me get a job in Arizona. Why didn't my sister in Nashville help me more?

I lean back in the airline seat and try to sleep. There is a guard sitting next to me reading a magazine. We do not speak to each other for eight hours. He will leave me in Guatemala City. From there I do not know what will happen. I have $15, American money.

There is no food served on this airplane. Only water. I drink three bottles. When I ask to use the toilet, the guard stands outside the door. Where am I going to go on this airplane? Looking in the mirror of the tiny bathroom, I see a skinny, weak man, and tears spring up again. My hair looks like a bristled toilet brush. I can't look into the mirror without crying. Or laughing.

We arrive in Guatemala City in the afternoon and a group of other deported men are escorted with me to a large white building at the edge of the airport. I hear marimba music playing on some loudspeakers and I stroll to the beat of the songs. A small grin lifts me from my sadness, and I thank God for the music of Guatemala. I smell the soft fragrance of gardenias mixed with gasoline fumes. I am home.

Immediately I get out of my jail shirt and pants and throw them in the trash. The prison returned one piece of Guatemalan identification, one jacket, my filthy jeans, a sweat-stained T-shirt, socks and torn shoes. The shoes have been ripped by the thorns of the desert. The socks are thick with sweat and dirt. I throw the socks away and put my bare feet in the mud-caked shoes. The jeans are stiff with cow manure from many months ago. They are the jeans Lester gave me. I smell like a barnyard and am disgusted by myself. Lester's jeans are better than the clothes from the jail. The smells of cow shit feel more honest than the prison pants.

Inside the building I am given a brown paper sack with food: a thick, cold tortilla with black beans mashed across the top, some potato chips, apple juice, and cookies. I wolf it down and am finished with the lunch in four minutes. It is the most delicious food I have eaten in months. Other men are stuffing the food inside their mouths like the wild *javelinas* I saw in the desert.

I am eventually called up to a desk and must prove I am Juan Carlos. My fingerprints are taken, and I am given *quetzales* in exchange for the $15 American dollars I have in my pocket.

Using a cell phone borrowed from one of the deported men, I call my home. My mother answers and begins to cry. We are both crying. My father will send me money for a bus ticket in the coming days, and I will complete the long journey back to my home and family. I can hear Lupita jumping up and down as my mother talks to me.

"It is *Papi*! It is *Papi*!"

Yes, it is *Papi*, and he is a sorry mess. But he is coming home. Maria cannot stop her tears, and we say very little on the phone. I just want to crawl into bed with Maria, the children, and the dog. I want to feel warm again.

Two days later I am in my village in the highlands. Everyone is standing on the front veranda of my father's house—my mother, father, brother, his wife, my beautiful Maria holding Lupita (squirming, trying to leap out of her arms), and Juanito, holding his favorite toy truck. I can smell Maria's black beans cooking in the kitchen. Fanning the coals of the cooking fire, a neighbor is preparing pieces of chicken and tortillas. To return home to such a fiesta is more than I had hoped.

Juanito has grown so much that his pants barely fit. He runs in his bare feet, which are tough like leather. Lupita is three years old and looks like a tiny Maria. Holding them both in my arms, we dance around the street in front of the house. Neighbors come out to see what all the commotion is about.

Papa calls us in to dinner, and he leads us all in a prayer of thanksgiving and gratefulness. I wonder why I ever left. The feast is laid before us, and I watch as my family looks at me. Everyone asks questions at once. What happened in *el desierto*? Did they hurt you in the American prison? You are nothing but skin and bones! Tell me about the airplane ride!

I am quiet during most of the dinner. The tears come again and I do my best to wipe my eyes when no one is looking. How can I explain all that has happened? The blackness of the desert nights when I was lost and cold in the snow seems like a distant dream. The wild pigs that pursued me, the vision of the Holy Mother when all was lost, and the home of Margarita and her husband—it is more than I can explain at this moment. These stories will have to wait.

For now it is enough to fill my belly with Maria's delicious tortillas and beans.

EIGHTEEN

═══ • ═══

Surviving

Margarita

AND THEN THE phone calls from Guatemala begin.

"¡*Hola, Margarita! ¿Como estas?*" It is Juan Carlos, and we quickly fall into our communication patterns. I speak Spanish; J.C. answers in English. We both want to practice our conjugations and tenses. My days in Alamos have helped my conversational skills, but I am definitely not fluent.

Juan Carlos is back in his village, and he sounds upbeat. Working for his father, a teacher, he drives a school bus every day. Some days J.C. works on the steep hills of the coffee fields, tying himself to the earth with a stake so he won't tumble down the embankments. He plants the coffee, tends the plants, and then harvests the beans. The work is sporadic. Sometimes he doesn't get paid.

"Some days they need twelve men, and twenty of us show up. I don't get chosen every day."

"So are you safe in your village?" I ask. "Have things changed?"

"Oh yes. It is much safer. We are guarding the entrance to my village twenty-four hours a day. There are no more drugs. My children can go to school. The biggest problem is that there is no work."

Woven somewhere into our conversation, there is always this invitation: "You must come to visit me and my family, Margarita. My parents send you blessings and prayers."

Juan Carlos asks about my husband, the dogs, the desert, the weather, his sister in Nashville, and *la migra*. He begins each phone call with, "What are you doing at this moment?" I am always taken aback by this question and try to paint a picture of my day.

"I'm sitting at my computer writing."

"I'm getting ready to go to band practice where I play the timpani in a band."

"I'm chopping tomatoes for supper."

It seems so trivial and banal compared with J.C.'s labor in the coffee fields, working long hours, often for no pay. J.C. knows very little about my life and how I spend my time, and I know so little about him. We both have the superficial facts but know next to nothing about what we do, how we think, whom we love.

And yet I have more of a glimpse of Juan Carlos in many ways than he has of me. I saw him in a state of fragility where words just got in the way. He was at the lowest point in his young life. He was close to dying, thousands of miles from the people who love him. He was vulnerable, weak, and brave.

Now he is struggling to find enough work to support his family, but basically he sounds glad to be home. I hear children shrieking in the background and dogs barking. A parrot or some other type of bird is squawking. There is life on the other end of the phone, and it sounds happy and chaotic. It's the sound of a young family, with nonstop chatter.

"I am living with my parents and my brother and his family. It is not good. I need to find another place, but I have no money. Would it be possible for you to help me out with the tuition for my son's school?"

And so it begins. Sending a small amount of money each month assuages my guilt about not knowing how to help this man when he landed on our doorstep months ago. It feels absolutely right to do this, and I wish I could send a larger amount.

In the months that follow, I become a familiar customer at the local Western Union office in a nearby grocery store. Sharing the line with customers who buy sheaves of lottery tickets, I fill out the necessary papers and send J.C. money each month. One time the cashier looks at my papers and tells me sternly, "I'm sorry, but we're not sending money to anyone in Mexico now."

"What?!"

She scrutinizes me as if I'm trying to send money for drugs or weapons or espionage. Her attitude annoys me. I feel like I'm being scolded for doing something wrong. Plus, who said anything about Mexico? My money is going to Guatemala.

After informing the cashier that I want to send money to Guatemala, not Mexico, she apologizes. "Oh, I just assumed you were sending this to Mexico. That's what usually happens around here. I didn't read your papers carefully."

She has a look of disapproval and impatience, and her tight-lipped responses to my questions are not customer-friendly. She rolls her eyes in exasperation, and the queue behind me grows. I am being judged, no doubt about it.

"So why aren't you honoring cash stipends to Mexico today?" I ask.

The cashier shrugs, and replies that it's a State Department directive. No money can be sent to Mexico today.

"Things may change tomorrow. This happens all the time," she continues, like one who knows the ropes. Her tone implies that I am naive to question any business transaction that involves Mexico. It's all questionable and probably tainted with something illegal.

The line behind me grows still more. Customers have their lottery tickets in hand and are clearly annoyed that I'm holding up their transactions. There is a hint of "grocery cart" rage in the air. One woman leaves in a huff, muttering under her breath about "going elsewhere to shop." Our transaction is finally completed, and I'm on my way.

Sending money to Guatemala is the first step. The next and most important step is calling Juan Carlos and giving him the necessary code numbers so he can retrieve the money. This is always a challenge. Often the phone connection is poor, and we struggle to communicate over the crackles and disconnects. His cell phone only works in certain places in his house or somewhere out on the street. His voice often breaks up. We struggle to hear each other. Sometimes there's rain, thunder, or wind. Reception is sketchy.

I tell him the ten important numbers he must write down in order to pick up the cash from Western Union. More often than not, we're disconnected in the middle of my recitation. I call him back and repeat the important numbers. He misunderstands the string of numbers. I repeat. He recites the numbers back to me. And so it goes.

Conversations begin and end with "*Dios te bendiga a ti y a tu familia.*" God bless you and your family. J.C. and his family attend the village Seventh-day Adventist Church—the evangelicals are a major presence throughout Latin America—so we never talk to each other on Saturday, as this is church day for the family.

I'm always the one to end our conversations. I simply run out of things to say. My Spanish vocabulary is spent. When he asks what I am doing, I answer, "I'm fixing dinner for my husband," or "I must go to town before the stores close." Truth be told, these are excuses. His life seems so far away, and my life is so very different from his struggle for food and safety that it's difficult for me to connect at a deeper level.

Email communication is sporadic. J.C. doesn't have a personal computer, and I never know when he's at an Internet café and can email me. Occasionally I receive emails with photos of his children and himself. I notice that J.C. has gained weight and looks more muscular. This pleases me. He looks healthy and proud of his family.

Before I call him, I sit with my Spanish-English dictionary on my lap and plot out what I need to say ahead of time. We are a comedy of errors. I speak in my bare-bones Spanish, and J.C. answers in English. We manage. And somehow we stayed connected.

During most of our phone conversations, at least once he asks me to come to Guatemala and visit him in his village. He is insistent about this.

"Please come during *Semana Santa*. I want you to meet my family." *Semana Santa,* or Holy Week, is Easter week in Latin America, the most important religious holiday of the year. It is a week of reliving the last days of Christ, with pageants, processions, special foods, and music.

Brushing aside this invitation, I don't consider it. The U.S. State Department would have me believe Guatemala is one of the most dangerous countries in the world. It's 2014 and the violence and corruption throughout the country makes headlines every day. Society in this war-torn country is on the verge of collapse. State Department directives are issued daily with travel warnings.

I only half believe them, but pay attention. After all, I live on the border of Mexico and the United States and walk into Nogales, Sonora, weekly. I know media hype when I see it. Parts of Latin America are not safe. There is corruption, violence and poverty. But I also know that other parts of Central America are incredibly beautiful, secure, and inviting.

I begin thinking about Guatemala, wondering if I could somehow make the trip and meet J.C.'s family, see his village, and also experience the vibrant culture and colors of Guatemala, the gem of Central America. J.C. is planting seeds, and I dream of visiting his homeland and somehow finding my way to his village.

THERE ARE MANY calls from J.C., especially during a crisis. And there are a lot of crises. Money is tight, and so J.C. calls to tell me of a plan to travel to Chiapas, Mexico, with his brother, to sell the textiles and crafts of Guatemala. He needs money to do this. He pleads with me to help him with this project. I can't do this and set my boundaries. I don't have the kind of money he needs to set up a shop in Chiapas, many miles from his village. Even if I did have the money, the plan just doesn't feel right to me. He would be leaving his wife and young children again. I encourage him to figure something out in his own village.

Two days later I receive an email from J.C. apologizing for his behavior. He's desperate and trying to figure out how to financially support his family. I don't have a clue how to help him. Personally, I hate advice, especially when I don't ask for it. J.C. vents his frustration and lack of financial resources, but he never asks me for advice. And I don't give it. He's thousands of miles away, and there's nothing I can really do but listen and just be there as he talks of his setbacks. I learn to be a silent presence on the other end of the line.

I know I'm getting caught up in a codependency web. J.C. calls when he needs money; I send him money because I don't know what else to do, and I feel guilty because I didn't do more when he was in my home. But I also believe in him; I believe he has the energy, discipline, and will to succeed somehow in his village. He is smart, driven, courageous, and has the tenacity of a survivor.

PART II

Guatemala

NINETEEN

Glimmer

Margarita

EVERY WEEK I continue to make the trek to an aid station in Nogales, Mexico, doing what I can to ameliorate the journey of the migrant. Of all the health care work I have done for the past forty years, this is by far the most challenging and rewarding. I am hungry to learn all I can to make a positive impact on the struggles of the migrants I meet. Meanwhile, the immigration policies of my country seem to make things worse. Instead of making progress toward immigration reform, the U.S. is becoming more punitive about the people fleeing their home countries.

I attend conferences and lectures and reach out to local activists and leaders. During the summer of 2012, I meet Sister Judy, an American Catholic nun and humanitarian activist in Douglas, Arizona. We meet in El Paso, Texas, at a conference about the "myths" of the border. She wears a hand-embroidered blouse from somewhere in Latin America and is sitting at a table taking copious notes. She's an attendee at the conference and looks like she's taking in everything she can at these seminars. A friend tells me that Judy spent many years in Guatemala during the civil wars of the 1980s and 1990s. When I introduce myself,

Judy invites me to come and visit her in Douglas, Arizona, where she is involved with a migrant station in Agua Prieta, a small town in Mexico just across the border.

Over the next few years, I stay with Judy in the convent of the Sisters of Notre Dame, often taking with me summer interns from various universities who are here for an immersion in the culture and politics of the border. The interns are sponsored by the Border Community Alliance, a nonprofit organization I support. We meet with Judy and her social activist cohorts. She tells me stories of living in the Guatemala highlands and navigating her way through phalanxes of military and guerrillas. Her disillusionment with the U.S. government and its support of the right-wing factions in Guatemala during those years is palpable. There's fire in her eyes when she speaks of U.S. involvement with the Guatemala military and the genocide of the *campesinos* (farmers). She was passionately committed to staying in her mountaintop village and doing what she could to support the people. In the highlands the temperatures were often below freezing at night, and the life was hardscrabble and difficult. Growing enough food was impossible. She talks often about villagers living on potatoes for weeks. Judy tells stories about walking for miles in the dark on a deserted mountain road in order to get needed supplies. In the middle of a civil war.

This woman is tough.

In the summer of 2014, on one of my sojourns to Douglas that includes an overnight stay with Sister Judy, I tell her about my friend from Guatemala, Juan Carlos, and my desire to track him down. We're sitting around in her living room with some of the interns and other sisters, drinking wine and eating some of Judy's home-baked bread. I tentatively ask Judy if she would consider going with me on a trip to Guatemala and paying a visit to a village in the mountains where the coffee grows.

Her eyes light up. She asks me questions about the geography and where exactly J.C.'s home is. I have no idea.

"He tells me he lives near a place called Colomba."

"Ahhh. That is near the coast in the west." We look at a map. It's near the city of Quetzaltenango.

"So," I ask, "do you want to go with me on this wild goose chase?"

Judy is definitely interested. We talk about going during *Semana Santa*. She tells me about the city of Antigua and the festivities held during Holy Week, the days before Easter. The murals created in the streets of Antigua during *Semana Santa* are made of flowers, sawdust, vegetables and fruit. Processions and music go on day and night.

I begin to think I can do this. I can travel to Guatemala with Sister Judy, who knows the country, speaks the language, and understands how to navigate the terrain. She will be my guide. We'll visit J.C. and then tour the country. We decide to take the plunge and be travel mates.

Over the next months, many emails fly back and forth. I pore over maps and Judy explains the distances between the mountains and cities. We'll travel by bus and shuttle, staying in small inns and hostels along the way. The *Lonely Planet* travel guide becomes our bible, and we agonize over which rooms sound the most charming and which prices we can afford. We'll travel for ten days, and the first part of the trip will be a visit with Juan Carlos.

I call J.C. and tell him of our plans several months in advance.

"So how far is your village from Xela?" I ask. Quetzaltenango, or Xela (the more common name), is the closest city to Colomba and the outlying agrarian village where Juan Carlos lives.

"Oh, it is maybe an hour or two. You must stay in my village for at least a week, Margarita."

"Is there a hotel or inn in your village?"

There is a pause.

"You can stay here with my family in our house. You do not need to stay anywhere else! We will have a special fiesta when you come."

There is a long silence as I ponder this invitation. I'm immediately anxious about staying in the home of my migrant friend. I'm contemplating traveling two thousand miles for this rendezvous with Juan Carlos, but he is still the "other." Suddenly I'm suspicious about visiting a remote village and a family I have never met. I barely know Juan Carlos. He is still a stranger to me. If J.C. fled Guatemala because of the violence, corruption, and poverty, how safe would two American women be?

I tell him this: "I will be traveling with a friend, and we will stay with you in your home for one day. We will stay in a hotel in Xela."

Guatemala City, the capital city, is our flight destination. It's considered to be one of the most dangerous and lawless cities in the world. I vacillate between seeing myself traveling to Guatemala and wanting to stay tucked in my own safe corner of southern Arizona. On one hand, I like to think of myself as a citizen of the world. This is my planet, and if I'm open and kind and curious, and use common sense, I'll be just fine.

On the other hand, I begin to envision the worst thing that could happen to me: I could get sick and die in some remote outpost, or Judy and I could be kidnapped and never heard from again.

Then I visualize the best thing that could happen: I could have the experience of a lifetime with J.C. and his family. It would be a chapter out of a Gabriel Garcia Marquez novel. I would be seeing the remote countryside of Guatemala and there would be no tourists. I would be living in a world of magical realism.

Magical realism wins.

In early January, 2015, while Judy is visiting my home on our ranch, we call Juan Carlos and discuss our fledgling plan. I hand the phone to Judy. Her Spanish is fluent, and she can more easily discuss the possibilities of where and when to meet J.C. Can we take a bus to his home? How will we get there? How difficult is the journey?

We hatch a plan: Juan Carlos will meet us in front of the cathedral in the main plaza of Xela at 8 a.m. on the Monday before Easter Sunday. He will drive us to his village and we will spend the day. J.C. tells us it's a short distance. He is excited, and speaks at a rapid-fire clip.

When I get back on the phone with J.C., I understand about one-third of the conversation, responding with affirmative murmurs and "okay's." I nod and tell him "yes, yes" when in reality I don't know what he's talking about. Thankfully, Judy is able to listen too, and she fills in the details.

When we hang up, I feel like this is one of those plans that have about a thousand holes in it. We may miss our rendezvous meeting place, our cell phones may not work, his truck may break down, we may be late, and I may fall and break a leg on my way to the main plaza in Xela. But it's all worth a shot. I really want to see for myself why J.C. fled his home, his young children, and his wife. I want to understand what it means to risk your life in a treacherous journey that takes you thousands of miles from your home to a country—my country—that profoundly despises your presence. At this moment I'm ready to take the plunge.

As much as I would like to stay a week with Juan Carlos and get a sense of his life, I realize that I know nothing about his village, his home, and travel in his country. Would we be in danger? Why didn't he answer my question about an inn or a hotel? Are there places to eat? Any restaurants?

Finally, I try to outline our travel plan. One thing becomes clear: J.C. wants us to remain in his village for longer than a day.

The months roll by quickly and soon it's spring and time for the Guatemala adventure. At dawn I meet Judy at the Tucson airport. She's carrying a thirty-pound backpack; I have a small backpack and a small piece of luggage that can be stashed in the plane's overhead bin. We're both two hours early.

March 2015

We arrive in Guatemala City at 10 p.m. The plan is to spend one night with two of the Sisters of Notre Dame who have lived in this city for over forty years. Their home is in a dangerous and forbidding part of the city, on the edge of neighborhoods where there is gang warfare.

Judy talks to a taxi driver at the airport, but he refuses to drive us to the convent. Too dangerous. She talks to another taxi driver, who also hesitates.

"I will take you one or two blocks from the convent and drop you off. You'll have to walk the rest of the way."

Judy looks at the taxi driver incredulously. "But it's late at night. We are two older women with luggage. Why can't you drive us to the door of the home of two nuns?"

The driver hesitates and takes a deep breath in exasperation.

"Get in. I'll get you there."

We pile backpacks and luggage into a decrepit taxi smelling of stale tobacco and burning motor oil. The trip takes us around many corners and darkened streets. The driver gets lost or confused or perhaps has second thoughts about delivering us to our destination. It's stuffy and hot in the back seat, and I'm exhausted. Opening the car window, I smell the night air, a muggy mix of car exhaust and smoke from open fires of street-side *taquerias*. Small groups of men in baggy low-slung pants and women in mini-skirts and platform heels loiter on street corners. Salsa music drifts through apartment windows. There is loud laughter and friendly tussling among the men. The women are smoking and gazing at the cab as we wind around the blocks looking for the address.

At last we pull up to a dark doorway and two sisters step out to greet us on the empty street. We pay the cab driver and he hurriedly lifts our luggage from the trunk, drops the bags on the sidewalk, and speeds off, kicking up dust as he deserts us. The two sisters have warm hugs for Judy, and we're ushered into the venerable old building where they have made their home.

Dragging my luggage into a vestibule, I see in the dim light many rooms surrounding a central courtyard of flowering plants and garden statuary. The sisters prepare hot tea and a late-night supper for the weary guests. We tell the nuns of our reluctant, timid cabbie, and they both laugh. One sister has served this neighborhood for over forty years and walks the streets every day without fear. She smiles and tells me that the women across the street will wake me in the morning with the slap-slap-slap of their tortilla-making business.

Gratefully, I sleep soundly and am awakened at five in the morning before sunrise. At first I think I'm hearing people clapping their hands, but I'm wrong. It is indeed the rhythmic staccato slapping of hands creating the thick tortillas of Guatemala. Slap. Slap. Slap.

Women are laughing and a baby is crying. People are lining up to purchase tortillas from this entrepreneurial street business. Toddlers clutching at their mother's knees and infants swaddled in *rebozos* (shawls) on their *mamacitas'* backs gather outside our bedroom window. We are in Guatemala City, a dangerous place according to the U.S. State Department and the mainstream media. And yet life goes on, with babies and children and women greeting the morning with breakfast tortillas. There's barely enough light to see, and yet school-children are playing soccer in the street, with lively music on the radio filling the pre-dawn air. .

After a light meal of warm, fresh tortillas, bananas, and yogurt, we thank the sisters for their hospitality, pack up our bags, and head to the bus station. Our plan is to catch the bus to Xela today and meet Juan Carlos tomorrow morning.

TWENTY

> ══════ • ══════

Small Miracles

Margarita

THE BUS STATION is alive with travelers waiting to be ticketed. We crowd into a waiting area and are jostled around by impatient customers. Judy motions to me to keep a sharp eye on my bags. There is an air of tension and possible danger in the bus station, and I try to keep my hands on my luggage and backpack at all times. Men stare at us curiously. We are the only *gringas* in the station.

There is one other woman in the station, and she has a young boy, perhaps five years old, hanging onto her skirt. She smiles at me and begins to speak English, asking where I'm from. New York is her home, and she's traveling throughout Central America with her son. Explaining that she was born in Guatemala, she wants to introduce her son to her native culture.

I immediately relax and feel a kinship with this woman and her young son. I figure if she can navigate the country with no real itinerary— she explains to me how they will camp and meander and travel with no reservations or hotel bookings—well, Sister Judy and I will be just fine. We have inns and hostels booked for the next ten days. And Judy knows the geography and sights to explore. Plus, her Spanish fluency will get us over all the bumps in the road.

We purchase our tickets to Xela, and settle into the rhythm of a long bus ride. Passengers unpack their lunches and children nap on mothers' laps. The women in their colorful hand-woven *rebozos* wrap their children close, and there is no crying or whimpering.

I watch villages and small farms whisk by as we careen along the narrow roads. There are no shoulders on the highways of Guatemala, and I take deep breaths as the bus comes close to the road's edge. The drop appears to be hundreds of feet. Judy tells me the names of the various villages as we speed through the countryside. Trying to pay attention to Judy's geography lesson, I nevertheless can't take my eyes off the cliffs and the steep drop-offs. The trip is a lesson in letting go of my disaster-prone imagination and enjoying the adventure. Easier said than done.

I realize that I am very dependent on Sister Judy, and am grateful that she knows the country and can navigate this journey. I hate being dependent on others for my safety and welfare but swallow my pride so Judy can take charge. My Spanish is of the floundering and grandiose hand movement variety, and my knowledge of Guatemala geography is nil. Lucky for me, Judy knows her way around this fascinating country and is eager to share her insights with me.

Some of those insights are grim. She points out villages where people were tortured in basements and their bodies never recovered. Some of them were nuns. I hear about her drives through the mountains in the middle of the night, trying to procure food and other supplies for her village. Often she encountered soldiers, and wasn't sure if they were part of the military or guerrillas. The guerrillas were her friends and comrades; the U.S.-backed military and government officials were not. She knew how to talk her way out of most situations, and probably played the "nun card" when necessary. During her time of service in Guatemala, she was always packed and ready to leave within minutes in case she had to flee for her life.

Judy has a sense of both caution and adventure. I appreciate this balance and so let go of my concerns and paranoia and sit back to enjoy the ride. The bus passengers are mostly women and children, and they murmur softly as the bus speeds along. A few have ear-buds connected to their phones and are listening to music.

We stop for lunch and I sample my first typical roadside offering: thick corn tortillas that look more like pancakes, perfectly ripened mangoes, and scrambled eggs. The salsa is mild, the tortillas are warm, and the coffee is hot and robust. I have to hurry through the meal—we have twenty minutes until the bus departs. And then there's the long line for the toilet. I worry that the bus will leave without me.

The bus driver is a kindly fellow with a bushy mustache. He helps me up the steep stairs of the bus, and I feel like an old lady. Suddenly I realize that I'm probably the oldest woman on the bus. Great. With my white hair and obvious *gringa* persona, I can rest assured that I won't be left behind.

Several hours later we reach Xela, where we hail a taxi that takes us to our small inn. Our lodging place has seven guest rooms, and the courtyard is a wonderland of flowering vines and balconies dripping with bougainvillea and jasmine. A woman greets us with a smile, her ebony hair combed into a thick shining braid hanging to her waist. The inner courtyard is private and enclosed, a refuge from the city streets. Pots of succulents are placed throughout the balconies and walkways outside each room. A young woman is juicing a pile of oranges into a colorful glass pitcher in the outdoor kitchen. When she offers me a glass of freshly squeezed juice, I'm sure I've entered a Garden of Eden. Our room is thirty American dollars per night, and that includes breakfast.

We settle into our quarters. The room is immaculate, with bright red handwoven spreads covering the two beds. Local folk art adorns the walls, and a painting of St. Bartholomew hangs above my bed. There are several electrical outlets for our cell phones and we immediately tinker with the Wi-Fi networking. I check to see if there are any messages from Juan Carlos.

Indeed, there are several messages from him. "I will meet you at eight in the morning by the cathedral on the central *zocalo*." The *zocalo* is the main plaza of the city.

My sleep is fitful that night, and I wake up both anxious and eager for this reunion. I have trouble remembering what Juan Carlos looks like. It's been thirteen months since our last time together, and I mentally rehearse how this morning will go.

Will he show up? How will we travel to his home village? Does he have his own car, or will we pay a shuttle driver to transport us? I have gifts for the children and the family. Is this an appropriate gesture? I guessed about sizes of clothing for his two children and I hope they will like the outfits—a twirly party dress for his daughter and some cargo shorts and a polo shirt with the University of Arizona insignia for his son.

I consider another possibility: J.C. doesn't meet us. Well then, Judy and I will explore the city and take in some of the Easter festivities.

Or he meets us but can't pay for a shuttle or a bus to transport us to his village and home. Okay, we'll pay for this and we'll stop by a nearby bank for the local currency, quetzales.

Or he meets us and we pile into his vehicle, and we break down in the middle of the jungle. For days. Surrounded by drug cartel gangs with guns and machetes, no one ever hears from us again.

Or he meets us at the appointed time and place. There are bells and whistles and jubilant greetings. We pile into his car and arrive at his village in an hour. It's a smooth and safe journey to the highlands of his home.

In the morning, I stuff the gifts for the family inside my backpack and Judy and I walk the few blocks to the cathedral. We arrive at the plaza one-half hour early. There is a *Semana Santa* procession lining up on this Tuesday of Holy Week. Women and children are dressed in traditional festive costumes; men are getting ready to hoist a huge *anda* on their shoulders. An *anda* is a large platform without wheels that's carried by the people of the villages during special festivals. The *anda* has several statues of angels, saints, a suffering Jesus, and his mother, Mary, gazing upon the faithful parishioners.

The plaza is crowded with children, families, dogs, and vendors selling special candies and pastries, as befits this Holy Week. I watch musicians playing a rhythmic tune on three large marimbas. They literally dance in front of their instruments as they harmonize the soprano, alto and bass melodies. As a mallet player in a concert band in Arizona, I want to join them and try my skills at this early morning improvisational performance in the *zocalo*. I could stay in this plaza the entire ten days and play music with the marimba players.

In fact, I want to ditch this whole crazy idea and just be a tourist with no commitments. Clearly I'm nervous about this meeting with Juan Carlos.

Cars circle the plaza slowly. I scan the crowds looking for J.C. and enter the church. Did I say I'd be in front of the church? Or inside? Or at the side? Or on the cathedral steps? Judy and I pace back and forth, looking for a Guatemalan man with short black hair, and we see hundreds of young men who fit this description. I go inside the church and there is a special mass being sung. Silently, I say a prayer that J.C. will find us in this throng of people.

It's 8:20 a.m. and I'm beginning to wonder if this meeting will happen. At 8:30 I text him, though I'm not sure he has a phone that accepts a text message. At 8:40 I receive a message: "Where are you? I am in front of the church."

I scan the plaza, and look carefully for a twenty-nine-year-old man in front of the cathedral. I see no one.

"Maybe he's in front of one of the other churches," Judy says.

We are in the central plaza at the *Catedral del Espiritu Santo*. There are dozens of cathedrals in Xela. Who knows where J.C. could be waiting?

Judy texts J.C. with the name of the cathedral where we're posted, waiting and looking. He answers immediately. "I will be there in five minutes."

I pace in front of a cotton candy vendor. Children are burying their faces in the pink confection at 8:40 in the morning. Young girls are dressed in delicate white frocks, and I wonder if they've celebrated their first communion. It's all stimulating and lively, and I'm continually distracted from the task at hand. I must locate Juan Carlos.

Suddenly I see a figure burst through the crowd, followed by a young woman and two young children. He strides across the street with confidence and joy and embraces me in an enthusiastic hug. There's muscle and flesh on his frame. This is a different Juan Carlos from the man I remember at the prison.

"Margarita! It is really you! We were waiting at the other church!"

Then the young woman, his wife, throws her arms around me in a huge hug as if she has known me for years. "*¡Bienvenidas!* God bless you for making this journey."

Then the children each give me a big hug, and Juan Carlos introduces me to his handsome family.

"This is Maria, *mi esposa*. And my son, Juanito. *Mi hija* is Lupita." The children dance around me like I'm the visiting queen.

I introduce Sister Judy, and she chats with all of them in Spanish about their journey and the mix-up regarding our meeting place. It's all unimportant. We are together, and now the real adventure begins.

J.C. runs to retrieve his pickup truck, which is double-parked, and Maria and the children pile into the back, while Judy and I are told to sit in the cab with J.C.

"Oh no! Please, you sit up front with the children and we'll sit in the back," Judy suggests to Maria. But it's too late. Maria and the children, ages 3 and 5, are already settling into the back trailer on a blanket. It's a chilly morning and I'm concerned about their comfort bouncing around in the back.

Well-used, dented and partially rusted, the white pickup truck has seen many miles. I climb into the cab and maneuver my legs beside the gear shift, and Judy rides shotgun. As J.C. grinds the gears, I am acutely aware that I haven't been this physically close to him, with our shoulders and legs touching, and I find myself moving toward Judy as much as I can. We're squished in the cab, and will be for a long period. J.C. is a total gentleman and apologizes for the cramped quarters.

Taking a deep breath, I relax into the moment and do my best to enjoy the ride. We are in Guatemala, and I am simply amazed that I'm spending the next hours with Juan Carlos and his family.

Through crowded streets, J.C. maneuvers around honking vehicles, sleeping dogs and pedestrians on their way to the cathedral and Easter festivities. We're a fish swimming upstream—everyone appears to be going the opposite direction. But J.C. obviously knows his way around the city. I peek through the back window, and the kids are squealing with delight. Huddled against their mother, they wave at me through the window.

After bouncing along for an hour, we find ourselves in the countryside. "How much farther is your village?" Judy asks.

"Not far," replies Juan Carlos. "We go beyond the coffee fields where I work."

"But how far?"

"It is just a short trip."

Judy gives me a sideways glance and shrugs.

Then she leans forward to look at Juan Carlos directly. "I just want to make sure you understand that we must be back in Xela before dark.

Can we make it back in time?" Her voice is assertive and demands an answer.

"There is no problem. You can stay at my home if it gets too late." He gives us a huge grin.

This was not the right answer.

"I know how these visits can go," Judy says to me in English. "I've lived in Guatemala for years and I know these people. First we must meet the whole family. Then we have dinner. Then we must meet the neighbors and friends. These parties can go on for hours. Believe me, I know the hospitality of Guatemala."

I quietly explain to Judy that J.C. understands a lot of our English conversation. At this moment he's sucking on a can of Red Bull energy drink and looking straight ahead, dodging pot-holes and stray dogs napping on the road. His happiness permeates the cab of the truck. All things are possible. He is in command, and he's bursting with chatter and elation.

Judy repeats in Spanish that it's imperative that we return to Xela and our hotel before dark tonight. She is adamant about this.

And J.C. just smiles and nods. We're in it for the long haul, captive in this rickety truck and dependent on Juan Carlos as our guide and pilot.

We bounce along, and J.C. points out some of the villages and landmarks. He has something to say at each curve in the road. He is our Condé Nast guide.

"This town has no men," he says, pointing to a row of houses. "They have traveled to *los Estados Unidos* looking for work or they have disappeared or are dead. The town is run by women."

He points to a row of cinder block buildings with colorful blankets and tapestries hanging on a clothesline. Inexplicably he chuckles, shaking his head as he tells us that the towns are in better shape now without the men. Chickens, cows, and an occasional pig meander about the front yards. Barefoot children play in the muddy ditches, and women wave as we speed by. J.C. is talking nonstop, happy and excited about our visit. The Red Bull has kicked in.

Soon we're in the clouds and I feel like I'm in a dream, a state of magical realism fantasy. The mist shrouds the hillsides, and I see waterfalls pouring out of crevices through the cloud layers. The roads are steep. We pass above the clouds and then descend back into the mist, barely able to see ahead. J.C. stops for me to take photos, proud of the beauty of this jungle wildness.

"It is different than the desert of *los Estados Unidos*, eh, Margarita?"

The dirt road is barely passable, and we lurch in fits and starts. Unpredictable ruts cause abrupt turns as we swerve up the mountain. I'm feeling a little motion sickness and take a lot of deep breaths.

The forest is dense with vines and trees. Small clearings of banana palms and rows of coffee plants dot the steep hillsides. There is no way a person could walk through the impenetrable growth of so many trees covered in vines. We're in a subtropical forest, close to the ocean, and the trees act as a net, catching the clouds and capturing water to nurture this dense jungle. The clouds blow in from the ocean, encounter the mountains, and then drop their precipitation on the leafy, tangled web of green. The cloud forests are the living aquifers of Guatemala. This is the major water supply for the cities and villages. When I take a shower back in Xela tonight, the water is quite possibly from the streams and rivers created by these cloud forests, a hundred or more miles away.

Judy points out the ceiba tree, which produces kapok, the cotton-like fiber used for clothing and pillow stuffing. We see copal trees, which produce the sacred incense used in the mystical rituals of the Maya ceremonies we will be witnessing all this week. The sap of the copal tree is highly combustible, and sold in many of the markets throughout Guatemala.

I see varieties of agave cacti, similar to those in the desert of my Arizona home. Long, entangled columns of night-blooming cereus crawl around trees and shrubs like a thorny vine, some reaching twenty feet into the air. Trees are flanked by so many brambles and creepers that they are difficult to see. A walk through the jungle would necessitate a machete to bushwhack a path. I think about the routes of the drug cartels and wonder if they have to transport their product through all of this foliage.

Two hours pass, and my back and derrière are sore and stiff. I ask Juan Carlos how much farther to his village.

"Not far."

I peer out the back window. The children are asleep, snuggled against their mother, who's also asleep despite the bouncing and grinding of the truck.

Soon we're traveling along a stretch of road above the clouds. I can see small enclaves of houses clinging to the hillside on terraces of dirt and rock. The small communities are a half mile away, possibly farther.

J.C. slows the truck, leans out the window, and whistles a cadence of five or six notes. It's a curious constellation of notes, almost like a bird-call. He isn't whistling a song, but instead a mysterious arrangement of notes. To my amazement, someone in the distance answers the whistle. He does this strange whistle tune again and this time waves his arm out the window. Now the whistling answer is longer and more complicated. Curious and somewhat astonished at this musical communication, I look at J.C. He just shrugs.

"Are you contacting a friend?" I ask. He just smiles. Instead of answering, he stops at a waterfall beside the road and invites me to take a photograph. And I do.

We ride along in silence for a while, and I think to myself that no one will ever believe this experience. Here I am riding along in a rickety banged-up truck with a Guatemalan *campesino* who's sucking on a caffeine-laced energy drink, and whistling some sort of coded message out the window. And high above the clouds in another village, someone answers in his own whistle configuration. I squint out the window to try to see who this faraway person can be and only see jungle greenery and small shacks clinging to a cliff.

Soon we come to a small pueblo called Colomba. Cruising down the main business thoroughfare, J.C. again whistles several measures of notes that are neither a song nor a tune. It is more of a whistled Morse code. People whistle back at our truck as we pass several market venues, again responding in a complicated pattern of notes and rhythms—maybe ten or twelve notes. I've never heard anything quite like it. The whistles seem to come from shop-keepers on both sides of the street.

From watching old westerns on television in my youth, I recall the American Indians whistling to each other across the canyons, communicating the presence of invading pioneers or enemy soldiers. When I question J.C. further about his whistling language, he seems self-conscious about what I've witnessed, so I let it go. But I'm fascinated and want to know more about this.

When three hours have passed, the road becomes even more rutted and narrow. Long curves around steep mountain ravines ascend up and up. Men are planting seedlings of coffee plants in fields on terraced hillsides. They look like tiny inanimate dots on the landscape until I see them swing a trowel and scoop into the earth, and I realize that they are alive. Each one has a rope fastened around his waist, which in turn is tied to a stake in the plowed dirt. This keeps them from plummeting down the mountainside.

Juan Carlos tells me that he's often hired for the day to plant coffee and tend to the cultivation. It's dangerous backbreaking work. Sometimes he makes only three or four dollars per day, and sometimes he isn't paid at all.

He shakes his head in frustration as we bounce along. "I can't make enough to buy food and clothes for my family working on these coffee plantations," he laments.

My watch tells me it's almost high noon. We have been on the road to his village for three and a half hours.

"We are almost there," J.C. announces when he notices that I'm checking the time.

"That's what you've been saying for three hours," I reply.

He gives me another grin and a nonchalant shrug.

I'm on his turf, so I may as well relax and let go of my American time frame. We'll get there when we get there.

After fifteen minutes of potholes and bone-jarring bumps, we come to a closed metal gate guarded by a couple of men. They aren't in uniform and look like local villagers. We have arrived.

"My village was overrun with the military, gangs, and drug cartels a few years ago," J.C. explains. "But now the people who live here have run the gangs out, and we take turns guarding the entrance to the town. Now it is safe. We don't depend on the authorities. They are all corrupt."

All this is said in a matter-of-fact tone of acceptance. The people of the village can be trusted; the government and the authorities cannot. We take care of our own.

"My children go to school again, and my wife is no longer afraid. My father teaches at the school after a long absence because it was too dangerous. He teaches history and mathematics. Things are much better."

Judy has been dozing, and as she wakes and looks out the window, she looks relieved. We see homes, a Seventh-day Adventist church, and a small *tienda* selling vegetables and tortillas. I am reassured that we're almost to our destination. Maria and the two children are waking up in the back of the truck, still wrapped in blankets and each other. I'm impressed that there's been no crying, whining, or whimpering from the children. This is one rugged family.

There's more whistling, with J.C. evidently announcing our presence to his neighbors as we pass through the streets of this small village.

People watch from porches, their eyes following this dilapidated white truck with the *mujeres americanas* in the front seat and the small family bouncing in the back. It feels like we're either honored guests or representatives of white privilege. Probably a little of both.

TWENTY-ONE

Welcome

Juan Carlos

LOOKING AT MARGARITA and her friend, Judy, as I drive toward my village, I pinch myself to make sure this is all real. The home of my parents is very poor, with mattresses on the floor and clothes in cardboard boxes. I am worried that this will not be adequate for my American friends. My parents will be amazed by my visitors. They are still skeptical about the things I have told them, and sometimes treat me like a little boy making up tall tales.

During these past months, I have bored my family with my stories of *el desierto*. I have watched as my family's eyes glaze over or they look away. My parents do not believe me anymore; they leave the table and go watch TV. My wife yawns and goes to bed. Only my children ask me to tell the stories of the dogs and the helicopter again and again.

I am nervous about these special guests in my house and can feel my stomach churn. Wishing we had more chairs for the *americanas*, I hope they don't mind sitting on the bed or outside under the trees. Maria and my sister-in-law have been cooking for two days, preparing my favorite dishes. We are borrowing plates and glasses from the neighbors.

We are almost to my village, and I need another Red Bull to keep me going. We left our house at 4 a.m., and Maria and the children have been sleeping in the back of the truck for hours. I shake my head to stay focused on the road.

As we pass through the mountains and canyons, I whistle to my friends and relatives who live deep in the forest. I gladly whistle my joy and excitement about my American friends coming to visit me. Margarita looks puzzled when I greet my friends. My father taught me to communicate this way with our distant neighbors when I was a young boy. Only the men connect with each other by whistling, and we do it because we live so far apart. I can hear my friends greeting me with a whistle across the mountains several kilometers away. It works better than a cell phone, which doesn't have a signal most of the time anyway. I whistle that my friend from *los Estados Unidos* is here!

I say a quiet prayer to God for the blessings of this day. Margarita will see how I live and will play with my children. Maybe I can persuade her to stay for a week here in my village. I will try. I am grateful that she has come this far to meet my family.

This is the best day of my life.

TWENTY-TWO

— • —

Fiesta

Margarita

NAVIGATING THE DEEP crevices of a washed-out road, Juan Carlos parks his truck on a steep incline in front of a cinder block house. Turquoise-blue curtains splashed with yellow flowers flutter in the open windows. Three people stand in front of the covered porch to greet us. A large tan hound meanders around the truck and sniffs my feet as I get out of the car. Judy and I greet the entourage waiting for us, and Maria and the two children clamber off the truck bed like they've done this a hundred times. Juanito races up the street to greet other children, and Lupita clutches her mother's apron as we're introduced to the rest of the family.

Juan Carlos's parents extend their hands to us as we walk onto the front porch. J.C.'s sister-in-law, Cecilia, also greets us. J.C. introduces me to his mother, Alicia, and she grasps my hand and places her forehead on my outstretched palm. She is crying and speaking rapidly. Thankfully, Judy translates as needed.

"*Gracias, gracias,* thank you, thank you. God bless you a thousand times. You have brought my son back to me."

I am deeply touched by Alicia and her unabashed gratitude. His father, Humberto, shakes my hand warmly and nods his head as his wife weeps. Standing there awkwardly, I want to tell them of my ineptness in handling the situation so many months ago in the desert of Arizona. I could have done so much more, but operated out of ignorance and fear. If only I had known the proper attorney to call. If only I could have figured out the twisted and convoluted tangle of asylum laws.

But today Judy and I bask in the warmth and welcoming gestures of J.C. and his family. This is a family that knows how to give love. Juan Carlos belongs with his family, and perhaps it was a good thing that I didn't know how to work the system and was unable to deliver him to Nashville and his sister so many months ago.

We enter the house and I'm surprised to see how large it is, with many rooms extending across the width of the lot. The windows have no glass but are enclosed with wooden shutters. J.C. lives in one large room with his family; its walls dazzle with bright coral paint. It's a spacious room with cardboard boxes of clothes and toys neatly stacked in the corner, and a bright pink and blue spread covering the mattress. The mattress looks like a king size and sits on the floor. I see a lime-green macaw sitting in a tree outside the open bedroom window, and he screeches furiously as we enter the room.

The children spy the bundles I've carried into the house and I pull out some gifts. J.C., Maria, Lupita and Juanito are all sitting on the mattress, and I place the gifts beside the eager children. They both look to their dad for permission to open the packages, and when he nods, tissue paper and ribbons fly in the air. Lupita's eyes are round, black buttons as she sees the pink and white ruffled dress with lace and sparkles. She quickly pulls off her clothes and dons the frothy party dress. It is a perfect fit, and I'm delighted that she's delighted. Today she is a princess, and she pirouettes around the room like a ballerina.

Meanwhile, like little boys everywhere, Juanito is looking for a toy. After he inspects the bright red sporty polo shirt and the cargo shorts with lots of pockets, I give him another package, books from Arizona, written in both Spanish and English. One of the books is about the *javelinas* that roam the desert—the same *javelinas* that tormented his father when he was lost near my home. It is the Spanish version of *The Three Little Pigs*. His mouth droops in disappointment, and I see him looking through the shredded tissue paper for something else. Maybe a truck or a fire engine.

Juanito, the spitting image of his dad, wants none of this civility as we sit on the mattress surrounded by scraps of tissue paper and ribbons. Books and new clothes are not on his wish-list. His mother asks both children to say "thank you" to me, and like children everywhere, both oblige in a quiet, self-conscious fashion.

Dashing outside to play, Juanito leaves the gifts in a pile on the bed. He's off to do more exciting things than strut around the room in new clothes. Maria is delighted with the presents for the children and grabs my hands, nodding and repeating, "*Muchas gracias, muchas gracias.*" She appears to be on the verge of tears, and continues holding my hands, smiling and shaking her head in affirmation. I'm grateful for this moment, smiling and nodding. The family is so effusive in their gratitude that my Anglo reserve stands out in marked contrast. I manage to say "*de nada*" several times, pleased that they like the gifts.

J.C. and Maria present Judy and me with gifts as well—a bag of locally grown Guatemalan coffee from one of the nearby plantations, and a large glass jar of their own honey, harvested from the trees in the backyard. I open the jar and stick my finger in the honey and take a taste. It's tangy and sweet at the same time.

Juan Carlos points to the coconut palms in his yard and explains that the bees pollinate the flowers and produce the honey.

"So how do you get the honey?" I ask.

"I climb the trees and steal the honey from the bees when they are asleep. Sometimes I get stung, though." He laughs, eyes twinkling with merriment.

I see plantains growing in long bunches from trees. Plantains are green and are usually fried when eaten, tasting different than bananas. Often they are served along with black beans and tortillas. Looking out the window, I see plantain trees growing up to thirty feet tall.

Maria rises from the bed and prepares lemonade for all of us in her small kitchen, which is on one side of the room. There is a sink and a small stove, with pots and pans hanging from the wall. Sister Judy helps Maria pass out the glasses of cool lemonade, and I drink quickly, the sweetened drink dribbling down my chin. Privately I wonder if the water is potable; I look at Judy, and I think she's pondering the same thing. We smile at each other and enjoy our drink.

This is a party and we are the honored guests. At this moment I am so happy that we made this journey. The miracle of making this connection with this family from thousands of miles away, arising from the chance meeting of Juan Carlos sixteen months ago in the middle of the Sonoran Desert—well, it all makes me smile. He staggered onto the patio of my home in Arizona, and now here I am sipping lemonade with his wife and children, chatting with him about his life in this Guatemalan village.

Juan Carlos wants to show me the back-yard, which is crowded with chickens, chicken poop, cows, a small garden, and an outdoor kitchen and grill for cooking. There are baby chicks chirping after the mother hen, and the macaw is saying something to me in Spanish. Little Lupita skips ahead over the manure and mud, her new pink dress floating behind her, quickly becoming dotted with mud specks. Wrapping her arms around one of the cows—a yearling calf—and nuzzling him, she invites me to give the calf a kiss. I oblige, planting a kiss on the forehead of the gentle beast. He smells of straw and manure and sunshine.

J.C. is forging ahead on the steep path into the precipitous back-yard, which hangs on the side of a mountain. I hang on to the plantain tree trunks as I slip and slide down the muddy pathway. How do the cows keep their footing on this precipice? I look at them as they contentedly munch on dried grasses and scraps from the kitchen. We peer into the cow shed, the chicken coop, and the jungle beyond, shrouded in a mist of low-hanging clouds. It is an exotically beautiful spot, but I teeter on the sharp incline, struggling to keep my balance.

The homestead is humble, a mix of home-grown food and low-tech energy, with a smattering of high-tech cell phones, a television, and exposed electrical wiring. I suspect that the family eats a lot of chicken, beef, eggs and plantains, all of it raised on this small plot of land. The children look strong and healthy. Lupita excitedly points out her special "caves" and hiding places as we walk along. Small dolls and little toy trucks are scattered along the path. As Lupita climbs up one of the trees, I think that maybe a pair of jeans and some sneakers would have made more sense as a gift than the pink confection of ruffles and bows that I bought at Penney's.

———— • ————

THERE ARE SHOUTS from the kitchen on the cliff side of this steep plot of land. The women are preparing a dinner, and J.C. is needed to grill the meat outside on the open fire. Climbing back to the house, I watch as my friend carefully tends the fire, blowing on the coals until they're red hot. Little Lupita slowly fans the flames with coconut palm fronds, and her dad places the meat on the grill. Thin slabs of beef sputter and set off bright flares as they sizzle. I sit on a stump watching my friend manage the grilling while Lupita keeps the fire going with her fan. They are a team, quietly discussing the finer aspects of roasting the meat. I whip out my camera and both give me a huge grin.

Judy is in the kitchen keeping company with Maria, Alicia, and Cecilia. The smells from the meat, onions and chilies on the outside grill are intoxicating. Our last meal was more than five hours ago in Xela, and I am ready to eat. Maria is preparing the thick tortillas on the outdoor stove, and I watch as they are stacked on a plate like flapjacks, covered with a brightly colored towel.

At last we're called to dinner, and I help J.C. carry in platters of meat wrapped in tin foil. A long table covered in a red and white checkered tablecloth has been set up in Juan Carlos's room, and the grandparents, parents, two children, sister-in-law, Judy and I are invited to the feast. Crowded with steaming dishes of vegetables, meat and freshly made salsa, the table has barely enough room for the plates and silverware.

The women have been busy in the kitchen. There are black beans, mashed and then cooked down into a thick cylindrical loaf, ready to be sliced like meatloaf. A macaroni pasta salad with vegetables and greens sits in a large clay serving bowl, along with the grilled, thinly sliced beef, the salsa, and the mound of hearty tortillas. More lemonade completes the meal.

J.C. sits at the head of the table, and Maria sits on his left, close to the kitchen. Like mothers everywhere, she is up and down, running back and forth from the kitchen, with hardly a moment to take a bite. Little Lupita helps her mother dish up the food; Juanito is the last to join us, rushing in after racing up and down the street with his buddies. J.C.'s parents join Judy and me at the far end of the table. They quietly glance at us with shy smiles.

We all sit quietly for a moment, and I'm not sure what to expect. Does the family say grace or just dive into the feast? Am I supposed to say something? With Judy here to help me navigate the conversations and customs around the dinner table, I feel more confidence and settle into the flow of the afternoon. This is not my party; I am not in charge. It is a celebration orchestrated by my Guatemalan friend. I try to relax.

Juan Carlos leads us all in a quiet prayer of thanksgiving, with lots of blessings bestowed on Judy and me. Then we get down to the business of eating this sumptuous meal.

It's hot, it's humid, flies are buzzing about the table, and it's all good. The food is delicious. I drink deeply from the glass of lemonade. The conversation is lively, and the moment is special.

"I want to talk about my time in the desert and how I found the home of Margarita," J.C. says.

He begins recounting his journey into the United States: his encounters with *javelinas,* helicopters, a December snowfall, and his time in front of our fireplace in the mountains of southern Arizona. As he speaks of enduring frigid night temperatures huddled against a rock and of the rancher who chased him off with a gun, his mother begins to weep. His father drops his head silently. Maria motions for Juan Carlos to stop these stories, and looks at three-year-old Lupita, who is listening with rapt attention.

Juan Carlos keeps talking.

I ask for a pen and paper. I want to capture these stories and these moments at the dinner table. Maria rushes into another room and returns with a scrap of paper and a pencil. I take notes, lots of them, as J.C. gazes into the distance, remembering the epic journey that almost cost him his life. It's his healing process: Talking about the fears and horrors stabs a knife into the beast.

At one point during the story-telling, Alicia rises from her chair and stands behind me, placing her hands on my shoulders.

"I am grateful that you opened your door to my son," Judy translates. "God placed you in the path for my son to follow."

I turn around to give her a hug, and she grabs my hand and gets down on her knees. Once again I am silent and look to J.C. for help. I try to explain that I only did what anyone would do. With great dignity, Juan Carlos tells me that no, this is not what he experienced in the United

States. Most of the people he encountered chased him, brandished their weapons in his face, and wanted him dead or gone.

I get down on my knees beside Alicia, and we just hold on to each other for a moment. She is weeping, and I, so full of German and Anglo restraint, blink back the tears, wishing I could help this family in some profound way. Write them a huge check. Build them a beautiful home. At least learn the language. Keep them safe and busy and proud and productive.

Everyone is watching. We gently rock each other as we kneel on the concrete floor. We're both moving in another space and time. Finally we help each other up, two grandmothers trying our best to touch each other at some level of our being. We pick ourselves up off the floor. Alicia wipes her eyes with her apron.

I have no words.

And then Maria brightly announces that there is dessert. She presents a large bowl of a fruit medley, with cooked garbanzo beans and stewed bananas, mangoes, and almonds. Lupita passes out cups ready for some rich Guatemalan coffee. The dessert is very unusual and tasty, with the natural sweetness of the fruit complementing the meal perfectly.

As we sip our coffees and enjoy the dessert, Juan Carlos tells me of his dreams. I think about the coffees I've sipped in the bistros of American cities, with the confections and pastries and whipped cream, and realize that I will never forget this cup of coffee, or this moment.

TWENTY-THREE

===== • =====

A Business Plan

Juan Carlos

MARGARITA IS WRITING down many things as I talk about my seven days lost in the desert. And then there are my endless months in the American prison, waiting, waiting, waiting for a glimpse of hope for a life in Nashville with my sister.

"So why are you writing all of this down?" I ask her. "I have done nothing important except to get caught in your laws and get deported back to my home, where there is no work."

"Maybe I'll write a book about you," she answers, "and I want to get it right."

I smile and only half believe her.

"So will you have it translated into Spanish?"

"I'll try to do that."

"But why write about us? We're just a poor family in the mountains, and I can't find work to support my children. It is the story of Guatemala, and everyone in this village."

Margarita does not answer my question. "So tell me about the work that you do."

I look at Margarita and think about her life in *los Estados Unidos*. She lives in a beautiful home with pure water coming out of the faucets, and toilets that flush. Food is crammed into cupboards and refrigerators. She has a small pond outside with little gold fish. Her dogs are fed three times a day. They don't eat scraps on the floor. I saw this. It looks like pictures in the magazines.

How can I explain my life here, living with my parents and my brother's family? I cannot make enough money to live in a separate house. Maria goes crazy living around my mother, who tells her what to do and how to do it. She constantly begs me to find another home for us. My father looks at me with frustration because I come home with no money after a day in the fields. There is no work for me here. How can I explain this to my rich American friend?

This is what I tell Margarita: "I drive a bus each day to the school, picking up the children, and then drive them back to their homes. I used to drive a bus in Guatemala City and Quetzaltenango, but there were men who took my money. They pointed guns to my head."

Maria looks at me with tears and shakes her head, silently asking me to stop talking.

"Sometimes I work in the coffee fields. Maybe ten men will show up to work and only four are chosen. Often I work all day pulling weeds and planting coffee, and I am paid maybe two or three dollars, American money. I can't support my family on two dollars a day."

Margarita watches me intently as she writes. Her friend, Judy, translates when I cannot think of the right words. I want to tell her my ideas, my dreams, but she will think they are stupid. No matter. I will tell her anyway.

She is writing furiously on the scrap of paper, and I cannot imagine what she is writing. At least she is listening. My family quit listening months ago.

"I want to open up a little store, a *tienda*, because there is nowhere to buy corn or sugar or flour in my village. People cannot buy food and supplies unless they drive for an hour to the next village. I will never be able to make enough money driving a bus or working on the coffee plantations."

Margarita looks up and listens to me. She stops writing.

"The *tienda* can be on the front porch. Maria and I can open a small store so people do not have to drive an hour for simple things—fruit, some vegetables, *harina de maíz* (corn meal), and salt."

"How much money would it take to open up a *tienda?*" she asks.

I have figured all of this out, and I have a list of things I would need to start a small business. I do not want to beg, but maybe she can help me. I take a deep breath and spit it out, looking my honored guest straight in the eye.

"I need five thousand dollars, American money. This will get me started."

Margarita is silent and writes down this figure. She is dressed all in blue, and there is a cross that hangs around her neck. She is a woman sent by God to help me. Her pants are the colors often used in the woven cloth of Guatemala. Her eyes are blue, and they stare at me as I speak. I walk a tightrope, trying not to beseech her about the money I need, and yet I would crawl a hundred miles on my knees to obtain the cash to begin my dream.

"I do not have five thousand dollars," she tells me. "I am not a rich person. But maybe I can ask my friends to help. Maybe I can get part of the cash that you need."

I let out a sigh. She did not say no, and she tried to say yes.

I smile and look down at the table. I think about all that has happened during this past year and all that I have not told my family or Margarita. There have been times when I have worked all day in the hot sun planting seedlings of coffee, a beautiful green plant that keeps the world awake with its flavors and smells. And then I have been kicked and insulted when I asked for my wages and told to wait a month and maybe I would receive the money owed to me.

There have been times when I have stayed in the bars in Colomba until dawn because I could not face Maria and the *niños* without my wages.

There have been times I could not fill my truck with gas and so did not go to work.

There have been times I never wanted to return to this house because I was a failure. A man who cannot find work and support his family is not a man. He is a parasite.

There have been times when I thought I would die, a bullet in my brain, as I drove a bus around Guatemala City and Xela, my cash purse full of *quetzales* and coins. Young men would board my bus and demand money, waving a pistol at me and sometimes at the passengers.

There have been times I wished I was dead.

And today we sit in this room, the table piled high with food, a table so full of food we cannot possibly finish all of it. I am trying to impress my American friends. I am poor, and Maria has prepared a feast that we cannot afford. I want to show them my life, my struggles, my family, and yet they tell me they must be back in the city of Xela before dark. Sister Judy keeps looking at her watch. The afternoon is getting late. I do not want them to leave.

I look quickly at Margarita's plate of uneaten food. She apologizes and tells me she cannot finish the portions. She nibbles at her dessert; she does not finish her coffee.

"Please, you must stay with us for a week. We are so grateful that you have come this long distance. You must not leave so soon."

I desperately want Margarita to stay with my family and understand the problems I face each day. And yet I am terrified she will do this and she will see the suffering and the hunger and the fighting with the children, with Maria, with my parents.

Margarita insists that she must go and we all rise from the table. There are many hugs from my parents, and Juanito and Lupita. I gulp another cup of coffee. It will be a long drive down the mountain for my guests.

I motion to Maria to save plates of uneaten food. Do not toss the food in the garbage. We will need it for tomorrow.

TWENTY-FOUR

══⟹ • ⟸══

Overload

Margarita

WHEN I WAS a little girl growing up on the South Side of Chicago, I would run outside to play after supper and my mother would always tell me, "Be home before dark." Leaving the village in the late afternoon, I remember my mother's admonitions. We must make it back to Xela before dark. Do not drive in Guatemala after the sun goes down.

After piling into the front cab of the truck, Judy and I settle ourselves once again, with me in the middle crunched up against the stick shift, Judy riding shotgun, and J.C. taking command of the wheel. I see Maria and the children climb aboard in the back of the truck and am surprised that they are joining us on the three-hour drive back down the mountain. Feeling appalled that we get the good seats up front while a woman and young children must ride in the open air in the back, I tell J.C. that I'm uncomfortable with this arrangement. Shrugging off my concerns, J.C. tells me that the family wants to accompany us on this journey back to Xela and our hotel. It's part of the plan. There is no use arguing about it.

So we start the whole bumpy ride back to the big city as the sun sets on this spring day during Holy Week. We're quiet on the return trip, and I doze off for a while, lulled into a light sleep by the droning of the engine and the curves of the road. The trip is long and arduous. A light nap mitigates my terror as we revisit the blind curves. I am spared looking at the steep drop-offs over cliffs of rock and tangled jungle vines. My trust is in the driver, and so far he's negotiated these mountain roads with confidence.

After a few hours, Maria knocks on the window of the cab and tells Juan Carlos that Lupita needs to go to the bathroom. J.C. stops at a small market and asks us if we'd like a cold drink. We climb out of the truck to stretch our legs, and J.C. returns with Cokes for us and a Red Bull energy drink for himself. After using the bathroom, the children climb back onto the truck where they're soon asleep on their mother's breast, wrapped in a blanket to keep out the late afternoon chill. Judy pulls out a bag of almonds, we sip our Cokes, and J.C. revs up the engine. He gulps down the highly caffeinated energy drink in three swallows, and we are on our way once again.

Five minutes later, the caffeine hits the talk centers in J.C.'s brain and he carries on a one-way conversation for the rest of the trip. I drift off, listening yet not listening. This is a position I often take when I'm struggling to understand the conversation that passes from Spanish to English and then back to Spanish again. He speaks once again of the towns we pass through that have no men.

"They are either dead or they left for *los Estados Unidos*" he remarks nonchalantly. "All the bars are closed and the streets are cleaned up. Maybe the towns are better this way." He grins.

I take in this fact. Towns in Guatemala have no men. I hear the words and yet my mind refuses to understand. I don't know how to process this conversation as we pass through these small villages, the houses with walls of brightly colored stucco and roofs of corrugated metal.

Women stand in doorways with arms folded, their aprons covered with embroidered flowers over simple cotton dresses. They sweep the sidewalk in front of their homes. They stare at me as we drive by, their eyes following the truck with the *norteamericanas*. The streets are immaculate. Not a scrap of paper or trash anywhere.

"The next time you come to visit, we will have a real feast that will last for days," J.C. says. "I want you to stay for many weeks." And on and on. I half listen and watch the blur of green foliage and terraced mountainsides of coffee plants stream by. I try to grab on to this extraordinary experience—the people, the ride through the jungle, the towns, and the arc of this relationship with my migrant friend. I cannot process all of it.

"When will you come to visit my family again?" J.C. asks me several times, "You must bring *su esposo* on the next visit." He asks where Judy and I will travel next during this *Semana Santa,* and I explain our plans: We will see the city of Antigua during the creating of the *alfombras*, the carpets of flowers and sawdust covering the streets during Holy Week. Afterwards we will spend time at Lake Atitlán and Panajachel, exploring the sights around the deep blue lake at the foot of a grand volcano.

At last we come into the city of Xela and the traffic increases exponentially. It is the week of Easter celebrations, and people are pouring into the city for the processions and festivities. We're stuck behind long lines of traffic, and there's gridlock at the traffic lights. Judy suggests that J.C. drop us off several blocks from our hotel and we'll walk the rest of the way. It's a good plan.

As we are dropped off in the middle of traffic, with cars blasting their horns and people jostling to get around us, J.C. tells me he'll try to "meet us somewhere again" during our holiday in Guatemala. Everyone piles out of the truck and there are quick hugs and good-byes. Drivers and pedestrians honk and shout with impatience as we hold up the lines of traffic. Juan Carlos ignores all of it.

"We will be traveling to many cities to see the *Semana Santa* celebrations," I say, as parcels and backpacks are wrestled out the door.

"Tell me the hotels where you will be staying and I will meet you there."

In a moment of confusion, with traffic and mayhem surrounding the truck, I tell him this: "I don't think meeting us is a good idea. We should say our good-byes now. I will talk with you soon by phone or email."

I'm blind-sided by J.C.'s plan to follow us on the rest of our Guatemala journey. But I do know this: I need some time and space to think about what comes next with J.C. and his family. Judy is out of earshot for much of this conversation, and I wonder if I'm missing some of our interaction, certain phrases lost in translation. Although I'm not absolutely clear, I think J.C. is proposing that he meet us somewhere in Guatemala and we all travel together. At least I think this is what he said.

Juan Carlos just gives me a grin, shrugs and opens the cab of the truck for Maria and the children. I watch as he eases into traffic and pulls away.

Judy and I slowly make our way back to the hotel, dodging the crowds and the dogs. Doing my best to keep up with Judy, I wind in and out of the throngs, keeping my eyes on my traveling companion, as I have no idea how to get back to the hotel.

I am fried. I want to find a quiet spot and shut off my brain for a while. As the streets of Xela light up with music and revelry and parades, I'm ready for a nap.

And I think about what this all means. Honestly, I don't want to see J.C. during the rest of my days in Guatemala. I'm exhausted after this visit. He doesn't have the money to follow me around the country. I don't have enough money to support him on this journey. And I don't have the all-embracing, expansive heart to invite him into my life during the next week of travel. I need some alone time, with no conversation and no endless truck rides on bumpy roads.

Judy has arranged many places for us to see, in numerous cities and hotels. I want to explore Guatemala without dealing with Juan Carlos's unfathomable problems. I want to be an American tourist and drink some fine wine in the evenings, taking in the color and pageantry of *Semana Santa*. After my visit to J.C.'s home and family, after this surreal day of travel to his village, after hugging his children and his wife, the life of Juan Carlos definitely falls into the category of the "other" for me. As much as I believe that diversity and embracing otherness make for a life of enrichment, I'm drained at this point and just want that which is familiar and easy.

I feel ashamed, weak, and full of white American privilege. At this moment in time, I'm spent. My mind is spinning. Fleetingly, I consider aborting our travel plans and just hanging with J.C. and his family.

But that fantasy fades away as I feel the vibe of *Semana Santa*. Here we are in the middle of Guatemala, getting ready to celebrate a week of Easter, and I'm ready for the party to begin. Judy and I have carefully plotted out the next eight days, and I feel a responsibility to stick to the game plan.

With the hot sun beating down on both of us, Judy and I slowly wend our way through curving streets back to our hotel in the late afternoon. I want to find a shady spot and drink a cold beer. Sounds of music fill the plaza. Four men standing side by side play two large marimbas for the festive crowd, and the intricate rhythms and mellow chords of the wooden keys soothe me. Standing idly by, I capture this moment mentally, and then I catch up with Sister Judy. Little girls in swishy ruffled skirts dance to the music as vendors stroll the sidewalks with colorful balloons, hand-woven friendship bracelets, and Easter breads.

Returning to our hotel, we retreat into our comfort zone—a comfortable inn and a clean, soft bed. We make arrangements to travel by shuttle to Lake Atitlán in the morning. I glance at my cell phone, noticing there are already three messages from Juan Carlos.

I respond, once again thanking him for the hospitality of his home and family.

At this moment, I turn away from the struggles of my Guatemalan friend. I find a quiet corner of the hotel balcony and I close my eyes and listen to the revelry and rhythms of the street.

TWENTY-FIVE

———⟹ • ⟸———

Spirit

Margarita

THAT NIGHT I sleep fitfully, with dreams of a macaw screaming in my ear. The next morning Judy and I climb aboard a shuttle van with eight other passengers, heading toward the famed Lake Atitlán.

After several hours of winding roads and a vertiginous descent into the village of Panajachel, the brilliant blue of Lake Atitlán comes into view, surrounded by three volcanoes—Tolimán, Atitlán and San Pedro. It takes my breath away. The lake is encircled by a necklace of tiny villages, each with its own crafts, art, and language. Judy explains that we can take a boat around the lake, stopping at the hamlets and observing the different textiles and customs of each place. We will stay among these enchanting villages for a few days and then travel on to Antigua and the Good Friday processions.

The largest town on the lake is Panajachel, or Pana, as the locals call it. Booths and tents are set up with artisans' wares from around the lake, and I'm back in shopping mode. The streets are alive with travelers from all over the planet, and I hear many languages as I browse the booths that line this lively marketplace.

The main street, Calle Santander, displays wares and food stalls from exotic corners of the globe, with black bean tacos, *pollo fritos* (fried chicken), pizza, and pan-Asian fusion cuisine. Judy and I eat our way down the main thoroughfare, and admire the colorful textiles of the region. Women with lustrous braids wrapped around their heads like crowns wear ribbons woven through the strands of hair. They show me their hand-woven wares, and Judy identifies which village they're from by looking at the colors and designs of the cloth.

When the Spanish *conquistadores* invaded Guatemala, the aggressive intruders demanded that the people in each village wear a particular color and clothing design. This was to ensure that the indigenous people could be easily spotted if they tried to run away from the master's landholdings. I'm so lucky to be with Judy on this trip. She's a walking, talking encyclopedia of information about the culture of Guatemala.

Many of the women still wear traditional *cortes* (skirts), *blusas*, (blouses) and *fajas* (wide belts). Some are in deep and varied shades of blues and purples; others are green with yellow and brown stripes. There is pride in the workmanship and designs of the textiles. Of course, the people are no longer forced to wear specific colors that identify their village, but many do out of respect for their history. I'm attracted to the blue and white designs of the women's skirts. The *blusas* are extraordinary, and I know I'll purchase at least one or more.

We make our way to our hotel room, which has a balcony situated around a lush garden filled with birds and flowering vines. Rather than finding a restaurant, we buy food from the carts on the street and a bottle of wine, and settle in for the evening on our little balcony. I'm seduced by all of it and never want to leave our roost.

My phone buzzes. It's Juan Carlos. I let it ring and decide to pick up his message later.

Right now I drink deeply of some decent red wine from Argentina and try to identify the birds flitting around the courtyard garden. The grilled chicken we bought is cooked to perfection, and the rice, black beans and thick warm tortillas complete the meal. We make a picnic of it on our balcony and are content in our little haven, watching the sun set behind the volcano on the other side of Lake Atitlán. Why would anyone want to leave this beautiful place?

Glancing at my phone, I see a couple of more texts from my migrant friend. He wants to make contact sometime during the next few days. I'll deal with this later.

Gazing at the tropical garden jungle in front of me, I sink into my patio lounge chair and nibble on a chicken leg. A woodpecker taps on a nearby palm tree, punctuating the evening silence.

I feel like a selfish shit, sitting here enjoying my supper and wine, but I can't think about the problems of my migrant friend. I need the quiet peace of this lovely spot to sort things out.

Later in the evening I text Juan Carlos: "We are in Pana. Leaving for Antigua in the morning. I need time to be alone during the rest of this journey. I want to think about ways to help you when I return to the U.S. I will never forget our time together."

J.C. responds, *"Dios te bendiga en tu viaje."* God bless you on your journey.

━━━ • ━━━

JUDY MAKES PLANS for the next leg of our journey. We will arrive in the ancient city of Antigua during the height of *Semana Santa* on Thursday, the eve of Good Friday. On Thursday night, we'll set our alarms for three in the morning so we can watch the creation of the *alfombras*, the carpets of color in the streets of Antigua.

Wait—3 a.m.? Judy has to be out of her mind.

She explains that the residents of Antigua spend the night designing vibrant tapestries on the streets, using special colored sawdust, pine needles, vegetables, and flowers, and that the art will be demolished by the processions of horses and people the following day. All automobiles are banned from the area surrounding the main plaza during the celebrations. So it is a night of people, art, and carpets of color in the streets.

I ponder getting out of bed in the middle of the night and wandering the streets in a country considered to be one of the most dangerous in the world. But with Sister Judy, anything is possible. I trust her judgment implicitly. She knows this country and has worked on issues involving race, gender, ethnicity, immigration, and sexual orientation. There's probably a halo of golden light surrounding her as she walks the walk of social justice. I need to trust the universe and fear no evil.

I inhale the rest of my red wine and close my eyes. Tonight I will watch the sun set behind the volcanoes of Lake Atitlán.

The next morning we travel by shuttle over mountain passes and through many villages to the jewel city of Guatemala—Antigua. Arriving at our simple hostel, we find our room, a spartan affair with walls painted coral, two twin beds with traditional handwoven bedspreads, one tiny window up near the ceiling, and a bathroom down the hall. Towels must be purchased at the front desk. The hostel is filled with young college students from all over the world. Room price: thirty dollars per night, including breakfast.

A small scruffy yard with puddles of water, scattered weeds, clouds of mosquitoes, and a couple of plastic tables is a gathering place for meals. I hear some soft guitar playing and discover an area with decent Wi-Fi reception. Everyone is hooked into their tablets and cell phones, intent on connecting with their respective worlds. We have left our bucolic balcony in Panajachel and are in the big city. It's definitely a different rhythm.

The showers are outside and the supply of hot water is sporadic. The clientele could all be my grandchildren, and most sport multiple tattoos and body piercings. Judy and I are easily the oldest patrons of this hostel, and the kids stare at us like we stepped onto the wrong stage in this drama. I settle into what could be a very interesting and stimulating time with the millennials. Since we're waking up at three in the morning, I'm not too worried about loud, partying college kids. We're going to be up most of the night anyway.

Tourists are pouring into the city by the thousands. We're lucky to have a place to lay our weary heads. Our room is clean, but the bathroom is full of discarded wet towels and soggy toilet paper, with strands of hair clogging the drains. No matter. We'll be wandering the streets most of the time; we're not here to sequester ourselves in our room.

I soak in the antiquity of narrow cobblestone streets and ancient crumbling buildings, many of them still showing damage from earthquakes that struck in 1773. On every street I see the ruins of historic architecture, with ornate Doric columns and delicate archways, all remnants of buildings destroyed in the massive temblor more than two centuries ago. We walk to the *Parque Central,* Antigua's center plaza, which is flanked by the facade of the sixteenth century Catedral de Santiago, and watch as the vendors set up their carts and tents in preparation for the processions of Good Friday. Judy tells me the parades will start at 4 a.m., and I want very much to see this spectacle. Spotting a coffee vendor and barista on the plaza, I hope he'll be offering up his brew in the early morning hours.

Judy takes me to her favorite café for supper on Thursday evening, a place where she studied Spanish when she was enrolled in one of the many language schools here in this beautiful city. During our dinner I hear the unmistakable beat of timpani backed up by majestic brass fanfares somewhere in the street—a small parade setting the stage for tomorrow's Good Friday commemoration. A band of musicians plays a slow dirge as the procession slowly advances along the street past our dining spot. Watching from the café balcony, I see a cavalcade of men in purple hooded robes leading another group of men carrying a long wooden platform, an *anda*. Forty or more men sway back and forth along the narrow street, carrying the heavy *anda*—an immense float carved in wood, with a larger-than-life statue of Jesus balanced on top. Jesus has the face of agony as he drags an enormous cross astride his shoulder. I stand on the balcony with a couple of young children, and we're speechless as we watch the drama pass by.

The evening dusk casts a magenta glow in the night sky, and the streets have a purple haze. The pungent odor of smoking copal, the traditional incense, rises from hanging coffee cans with holes punched in the sides and suspended from poles held by the faithful as they slowly lead the procession.

I return to the table to finish my dinner, but I can't eat. Inexplicably moved by this preliminary drama, I'm feeling withdrawn and introspective. And the real show hasn't even begun.

After our meal, there are men dressed in purple satin robes and head coverings walking the streets, all of them looking like they're on some sort of mission, going somewhere important. I can't decide whether I should follow them or return to the hotel for a few hours of sleep before our 3 a.m. wake-up call.

I choose the latter. Judy and I are old, and need our rest. Fortunately, when we return to the hostel, it's quiet and empty. Of course, the young patrons are out in the streets of Antigua enjoying the beginnings of the celebration.

My mind is buzzing with all I've seen. Throughout the night, I can hear the sounds of the drums and the brass bands playing their powerful funeral dirges. Or am I dreaming this? I sleep restlessly, and when the alarm goes off at three, I'm up and staggering about the room, pulling on some clothes, running a comb through my hair. Part of me wants to abandon this whole idea and crawl back into bed, but curiosity prevails. And adrenaline kicks in. I hope this doesn't turn out to be most insane thing I've ever done. Prowling the streets of Antigua in the dark could be dangerous. Or incredibly exciting.

We're the only ones in the hallway of our hostel, and the snores of guests echo up and down the passageway. When we hit the streets, the narrow avenues are crowded with people in long biblical robes and head-gear; men on horseback are dressed like Roman soldiers with silver helmets and spears. Some men wear purple pointed hats covering their faces, with strange eye holes in the front, looking like vestiges of the Ku Klux Klan. I feel like I've stumbled onto a movie set.

Children and parents are kneeling in the streets, sprinkling handfuls of tinted sawdust through stenciled cardboard templates of birds, flowers, and symbols of the Easter season. There are flashlights and headlamps to illuminate the work in the dark pre-dawn hours. It's a circus of activity.

My mouth is half open in astonishment. I'm walking the streets of Jerusalem in a time warp two thousand years ago. Roman soldiers atop horses prance up and down the cobblestone streets, their purple capes swooshing about their shoulders. Hooves clatter on the stones creating sparks. Their presence has a menacing quality, and I pay attention to my gait in order to stay out of their way. I feel like I'm being tossed out of the Garden of Gethsemane, surrounded by Roman soldiers and Judas; something momentous is about to happen. Forces of good and evil abound in the ancient streets. So much is going on that I frequently lose track of Judy in the darkness and am torn between watching the activity, or paying attention to my guide.

My cell phone is once again buzzing with a text message. It's Juan Carlos, and he wants to know where I am. He sends me blessings from God. In the dark I text him: "I am in the streets of Antigua watching the *Semana Santa* activities on this Good Friday." It's the middle of the night, and Juan Carlos wants to know what I'm doing. I'm both touched and puzzled by his insistent tracking of my whereabouts. There is such a cacophony of sound and activity around me that I can barely keep my wits about me.

"I will tell you about the processions later in the day," I text Juan Carlos.

Privately I'm relieved that he and his wife and the two children and his parents and the rest of the extended family are not with me at this moment. It's simply too much, and my disorientation in the middle of the night is just about all I can handle. I'm in another world and I'm loving it. It is enough.

Plus, I'm aware of my age. I am probably twenty years older than Juan Carlos's mother. I could be his grandmother. Looking around the crowds in the street, I realize I'm one of the older people wandering about in the middle of the night. I may feel like forty tonight, but the reality is this: I move slower, am mindful of where I put my feet, and am cautious about falling. These are things I never thought about thirty years ago. I say a prayer of gratitude tonight for being in this place of revelry and celebration.

Swept along with this crushing crowd of people, I am anonymous and safe in the obscurity of nighttime in the city. Judy warns me to keep track of my money and passport, as pickpockets take advantage of the crowds with cash in their pockets. I half listen. Who would commit a crime amid all this religious pageantry?

Spotting the barista on the corner of the plaza, I call out to Judy that I could use a cup of coffee. The small espresso bar is packed with people, and most are dressed in long satin robes and head scarves like monks from another century. They're sipping cappuccinos and taking photos with their cell phone cameras. Monks and priests dressed for another millennium are jostling for their coffees and catching up on Internet messages. It's incongruous.

I step up to the bar and order a café latte, watching the barista expertly steam the milk and pour it over my frothing cup of morning brew. Freshly ground Guatemalan coffee with steaming milk and a pinch of nutmeg is the perfect way to start off the morning. It's three-thirty, and as I feel the buzz of caffeine, life is just about perfect.

A woman in a beautiful red *huipil,* a blouse with embroidered birds and flowers, is selling warm *empanadas* (baked turnovers with fruit inside) fresh from the oven, and I watch her pile the pastries on a platter as she stands behind her cart at the edge of the plaza. I walk over with my cup of java and the smells coming from her venue are intoxicating. There are pineapple, squash and apple confections, and I ponder the choices for a moment before settling on pineapple. The vendor hands me an *empanada* in a small paper napkin, and the warmth and richness of the buttery crust soaks through to my fingertips.

I should get up at this hour more often. I'm energized and excited about my day.

Distant drum-rolls permeate the night air, and Judy and I hurry to get a decent spot on the street as the procession is about to begin. The crowd is densely packed, shoulder to shoulder, strangely quiet and reverent. Many hold candles. Children are hoisted onto the shoulders of fathers, while some little boys dash around the streets, their Nike tennis shoes peeking out beneath their robes. They look like the shepherds of two-thousand years ago, and the early hours of the morning have wired them. It is now four o'clock, and they're tearing around like little tornadoes, no parents in sight, having the time of their lives.

I smell the procession before I see it. The copal creeps through the streets in a pungent purple cloud, as boys swing small canisters of the burning incense. Slowly moving out of *La Merced Catedral* on the plaza, the *anda* enters the square. The ponderous, haunting march, with brass and drums creating a mournful dirge of suffering, silences the spectators. Munching on my warm *empanada* and sipping my coffee, I wait for the procession to pass by. I feel warm, safe, nurtured and alive. And very awake. It occurs to me that there is no police or military presence in the streets. I smile at this thought.

Carrying the huge *andas* is a feat of strength, grit, and will. The floats sway precariously back and forth, and I try not to visualize the huge platforms tumbling into the crowds. The *andas* swing in rhythm with the timpani pounding out the slow repetitive dirge. There are hundreds of men costumed in purple satin robes. They are called *cucuruchos*, and the color purple is significant of penance and suffering, a symbol of collective sorrow for one's sins. There are no cheers or laughter. The crowd contemplates the pain and suffering of the crucified Christ.

One of the *andas* is carried by women. This is the float with the Virgin Mary, gazing at her Son who is about to die on the cross. The women are dressed in black and wear white lacy veils. As their faces grimace and strain under the weight of the *anda*, they bear the burden of the blessed mother. Their expressions are solemn, focused and devoted. They are in another world.

The spectacle has an emotional impact on me that takes me by surprise. Whether you believe in the Christian story of suffering, redemption, and resurrection doesn't matter. There is something powerful going on here. The fusion of Mayan and Catholic rituals casts a spell over the thousands gathered in the early morning hours. People are in tears.

I am in tears.

This is a celebration of the passion and suffering of Christ. There is no joy on this day. I am not a person who dwells on the torturous journey of Christ's life. My idea of Easter is more in line with "Hallelujah, He is risen!" Followed up by a platter of deviled eggs and a honey-baked ham. I like the uplifting anthems of Handel's *Messiah*. I don't like to think about the Romans' peculiar brand of torture—nailing someone's hands and feet to a wooden cross and leaving him to die in agony.

But this is Guatemala. The facial expressions of the participants carrying the *andas* say it all. They grimace; beads of sweat appear on their foreheads. I can hear heavy breathing and groaning as they pass by. Their footsteps are leaden as they trudge along with the beat of the timpani.

The message carries the weight of two thousand years. The people of Guatemala live this message: Life is hard. Suffering is a part of it. We won't sugar-coat this. And we will persevere.

Soon the procession reaches the streets covered with *alfombras*, and the ornate carpets of vibrant colors are destroyed under the hooves of horses and the shuffling feet of the *cucuruchos*. The art and beauty of the *alfombras* are transitory, disappearing into the dust of the streets. It's all a symbol of the fleeting cycle of life. We are born, we flourish and create beauty, often we destroy, and we disappear into the earth. I wince as I watch the *alfombras* disintegrate, the beautiful birds and flowers of sawdust and pine needles tossed asunder. The procession marches over the creations; the streets are a shambles. Some of the artisans will reconstruct the *alfombras* tonight in preparation for tomorrow's parade. It truly takes the whole city to create this visual tapestry.

Standing on this street corner, I again start to think about my odyssey with Juan Carlos. He wants to spend more time with me during my visit to Guatemala. I'm not comfortable meeting him again. I'm not sure why. All I'm certain of is this: I need a break.

I really don't know how to rescue him from his circumstances, and this is an underlying theme between us. I am the helper; he is the helpee. He is an indigenous Mayan person living in the highlands of western Guatemala. I am an American woman living in southern Arizona on a quest to visit the village of my migrant friend. Feeling a deep connection with this person, I have embarked on this odyssey to find him and see for myself how he lives.

And now I need to separate myself from his struggles. My mind needs a break. My conscience is most definitely bothering me about all of this.

At this moment, I don't know how my comfortable world in Arizona can influence the life of this young man and his family. I live in the Arizona borderlands. Juan Carlos lives in Guatemala and is stuck in poverty hell.

I am enjoying some serenity standing here in the streets of Antigua, watching the processions creep by, sipping my latte and physically feeling the thunder of the timpani rolls. It's a kind of poetry that touches me as I stand in a new reality—a reality of mysticism and smoky incense and suffering faces.

I live in a world sheltered from so much pain and anguish. My Arizona home is in a beautiful canyon, and my pantry is crowded with too many jars and cans and boxes of food. I have coffee beans from four countries. I have money in the bank and a little to spare for trips such as this. I have never been truly hungry in my life. I have never had to run for my life.

Juan Carlos spends eight to ten hours a day working in the coffee fields or driving a bus in one of the most dangerous cities in the world. Often he is not paid. He is lucky to bring home twenty dollars a week. During my brief day with this family, his wife and in-laws looked at me like I was an angel descending from the heavens, a person who had rescued Juan Carlos from certain death. And now I will somehow fix their lives? I will offer some escape?

Of course this is an impossible task. And I am definitely no angel.

People ask, why do Guatemalans want to come to the United States? Guatemala is a beautiful, lush country. Judy says it's the jewel of Central America. She's right. Why would anyone leave?

Consider this: Juan Carlos lives in a cinder block home with his wife, his two young children, his parents, his brother and wife, and their two children. The house has several rooms; there are three families under one roof, and tempers inevitably flare. The grandparents rule the roost. J.C. never saves a dime. The children must pay for books and uniforms in order to go to school. If someone gets sick or injured, there's no money for medicine or a doctor. And then there is the corridor of drug trafficking, always a menace, and always the underbelly of everyday life. Just because you don't see it doesn't mean it isn't there. You never take a vacation. Almost everyone in your country lives the same way, and often worse. It's a hall of mirrors, like in the circus sideshows of my youth.

And then someone—a sister, a cousin, an aunt—migrates north to the United States and you hear of their life in the cities, in the farming communities, in the factories. Juan Carlos remembers living with his sister in Nashville. He recalls working in a Japanese restaurant, making sushi and yakisoba noodles. He was young and eager to learn, and he sent money back to his parents in Guatemala. For a while, things were working. But now he's back in his village with a wife and children. Things are different. And he's feeling stuck.

Dawn is lifting on this Good Friday morning. The sky is pink, and I see sunlight peeking through the edge of the urban landscape, reflecting on one of the volcanoes outside the city. Judy and I follow the procession through the streets and become a part of the passion play. We stop for some breakfast, and my phone buzzes. I answer. It's Juan Carlos, wishing me a blessed day in Antigua. I smile at the graciousness of my friend with his blessings and his prayers, and I'm ashamed that I'm avoiding him.

Juan Carlos and his family are better people than I will ever be. They offer their hearts to me and invite me to their table to share everything they have. I come up with all kinds of excuses about avoiding him, but here is the honest truth: I can't handle the ingenuous love and generosity of this humble family. The dynamics make me very uncomfortable. And I really don't know why.

TWENTY-SIX

Questions

Juan Carlos

I CAN'T STOP thinking about Margarita and her time in my home. Why did she leave so soon? I wanted her to stay for a month and show her my gratitude for saving me from certain death in the desert. She does not answer my phone messages. What am I doing wrong?

I discuss all of this with Maria. Maybe our dinner was not good enough. She left food on her plate. I will text her and say that next time we will prepare a feast that is ten times better than we served. There are no hotels in my village, but I will give her and Sister Judy my bed. We will take care of her like she took care of me.

We will visit the coffee plantation where I work sometimes. She will see how I spend my days on the steep hillsides, planting the coffee, picking the ripe beans, pulling the weeds. The owner of the plantation is from *los Estados Unidos*. Maybe she can talk with him about steady employment for me.

My father will introduce her to the teachers at the school and she will see him teaching mathematics and history to the children. My father is an educated man! I want my children to have a good education, and I am fortunate that my father is a teacher and is able to help Lupita and Juanito learn what is important.

I want to talk with Margarita again and explain so many things. I don't know how to ask her for help and yet I must. She has sent me money each month to help with school uniforms and medicines when my children were sick. Without her help I would have to leave again, and travel into Chiapas, Mexico, and possibly back to *los Estados Unidos*. I will do any kind of work to support my family, but the fact is, there is no work. There is no money. There is only corruption and poor wages.

I will call her again. Maybe this time she will answer. I must talk with her before she leaves Guatemala. Please, God, I pray for the day when I am not asking someone for money. I am humiliated when I do this, but I must earn enough money to feed my family.

TWENTY-SEVEN

=== • ===

Disparity

Margarita

THERE IS A blur of processions, mournful music on every corner, and throngs of people crowding the cobblestone streets, night and day. We walk, we watch, we eat, we sit on the curbside, we get lost a few times, and the intensity of these days of penitence and remembrance penetrates our souls.

I get a spot of gastrointestinal upset and keep a sharp eye out for all public restrooms. In one of my forays into a restaurant with a restroom, I meet a man, another American, who is also experiencing an upset stomach and intestinal urgency. We're both slightly embarrassed as we line up to use the one toilet. He admits that his malady is probably due to the cream-filled confections he's been eating on the street, but he doesn't want to give up and go back to the comfort of his hotel. And neither do I. We both chuckle at our predicament, use the facility, and head out to the streets again.

As I watch a parade showcasing an *anda* carrying a supine Jesus lying on a pallet, the clusters of people are especially close. Statues of angels surround the dead Jesus. It's the afternoon of Good Friday, the moment when Jesus has perished. It is an especially powerful moment, a climax to the day. I am literally lifted aloft a few inches by the tides of people craning to see the spectacle. Struggling to take some photos of the men carrying the *anda,* their faces contorted with grunts of effort in each step, a crowd of people dressed in indigenous hand-woven garments from their villages suddenly surrounds me. They are small people, less than five feet in height, and I step aside, allowing them to pass in front of me so they can have a better look. But they don't move. I feel several women pressing against me. I am tall by Guatemalan standards, and the women are tiny in stature. Totally focused on the parade, I ignore the pushing and shoving.

The moment passes. The crowd subsides. Fifteen minutes go by, and suddenly I see a young monk about fifty feet away waving a small wallet in the air.

"Who dropped their wallet?" he shouts. Idly watching him, I realize that it's my wallet! How did he get it?

"Hey, that's my wallet!" I gesture to him wildly, calling out to this purple-robed monk. I ask to see the wallet, still not believing it's mine. But indeed, it is mine and was taken from my cargo pants pocket, which was zipped shut. I am a victim of the notorious pickpockets that I have read about in our Guatemala guide books.

Frantically I search through the wallet to see what's missing. My passport, credit card, driver's license, and insurance information are intact. The money is missing—probably about forty dollars. Relieved and angry and stunned all at once, I thank the young monk for rescuing my property and am in a state of disbelief that someone could pry open a zipped pocket and steal my money.

"*¡Cuidado! ¡Dios te bendiga!*" (Be careful! God bless you!) my young monk rescuer calls out.

I'm shocked that people take advantage of such a holy, prayerful moment, the moment the *anda* carrying Jesus rolls by, the high point of Good Friday. A pox on these pickpocket thieves, whoever they are! May thunderbolts rain down on your heads! I'm angry and feel violated.

In one moment I have a taste of the desperation of the people around me. There is more going on here than religious devotion. The suffering goes beyond Jesus and the cross. Economic disparity is rampant in Guatemala. I am *una mujer rica*—a rich American woman. When there is no work, one must steal to survive. Or bribe. Or enter into relationships where there may be some monetary reward. Or die.

Later in the day I look for a church. Time to sit in a dark, cool sanctuary and just escape from the crowds and the noise for a while—this is what I need. At my core I am a reserved, quiet person. The crush of the masses is suffocating me at this moment.

I find an open door to one of the large cathedrals, and go inside for a breather. Sitting quietly in a church, looking at the statues and paintings, helps me regain my footing. A yellow hound dog snoozing in the aisle is my only companion, and this peaceful creature is my Good Friday gift.

I try to pray. I'm not sure what prayer is, really. I talk to myself constantly, and my inner chatter is often directed toward God or to something out there that I can't define. And usually comfort and calm follow my inner dialogues. Sitting in this church on this Holy Good Friday is my healing balm today. No sermons, no lessons to ponder, just the tranquility of this sacred space. The yellow hound licks my toes. I take a lot of deep breaths and once again walk into the crowded streets of Antigua, feeling refreshed.

Lying awake that night in our hostel, I hear the drums and the dirges that continue until dawn. The pageant goes on and on. It's hallucinatory, and I wander in and out of dreams filled with purple satin and grasping, starving people. I sleep fitfully, and Judy and I are ready to leave this beautiful city the next morning.

Glancing at my phone, I see several messages from Juan Carlos. He sends me many blessings from his family, thanking me for coming to his village to visit.

I need mental space to process what the next steps are for me and Juan Carlos. Plus, my gastrointestinal tract is definitely upset, and the bathroom has become my next best friend.

For the first time in weeks, I pray in a conscious way. I ask God for guidance and strength and equilibrium as I travel through the mountains of Guatemala. I ask for a quiet stomach and an open heart.

I text Juan Carlos and thank him again for his hospitality and good wishes.

WE WILL MOVE on to Chichicastenango (also known as Chichi) and the Indian markets. I am ready to shop. I am ready to leave the world of sin and penitence and move on to the world of the material. Judy assures me I won't be disappointed.

Clutching my canvas shoulder bag, I feel through the cloth to make sure that my passport and money purse are intact. Wary of anyone who crowds too close to me in the streets, I'm on hyper-alert, silently taking inventory of my backpack, my one piece of luggage, and my purse. They're never out of my sight. I've learned my lesson. I scan the street for an ATM machine to replenish my wallet with more *quetzales*. American consumerism is on the march. I'm ready for the market place.

We arrive in Chichi on Easter Sunday and are literally swept into the marketplace by a river of tourists and indigenous Mayans. The textiles and crafts dazzle in magentas, blues and purples. The day is dusty and hot, and the aisles are crowded with people in traditional Guatemalan dress and a fair smattering of gringos in straw hats and expensive sandals. Gringos have their cell phone cameras at the ready, while the Mayans are in a state of reverence and religious ecstasy. Trying to take in the mayhem and color, I'm dizzy from the chaos of the festival.

Explosions of firecrackers, or *bombas,* accompany drums and the trills of high-pitched flutes as a procession of the faithful takes over the main aisle of the market. Indigenous Mayans in frightening wooden masks pour into the marketplace, dancing to the thumping beat of the captivating ancient music. Men ignite wooden balls of firecrackers, shouting, *"¡Bomba!"* and dispersing the crowd before an ear-splitting blast shatters the air.

A man with a high-pitched wooden flute carries a large drum on his back. Another man follows closely behind him beating the cadence of the parade. Their music is electrifying, ancient, hypnotic. They are followed by men carrying *andas* covered in flowers and statues of the risen Christ. Women accompany the floats wearing folded cloths of brilliant colors on top of their heads.

I don't understand any of it and yet feel connected to all of it.

These are not shows for tourists, but rather a ritual that predates the Spanish conquest of the early 1500s. There is an odd mix of Christian saints and symbols, together with Mayan beliefs. The cross is symbolic of the four directions; Jesus is the Mayan father of the sun; Mary is the mother moon. The vertical bottom of the cross is the earth; the upper end is the sky. Elders, called *cofradias*, are members of a Christian brotherhood and are held in great esteem as they perform the liturgy in front of the church.

I stand on the steep steps of the Church of Santo Tomás, high above the market, and have managed to be in the middle of the *cofradias* as they set off the *bombas* and carry the *andas* into the ancient edifice. I'm trapped here along with a few other gringos who, like me, don't understand what is going on. As the *cofradias* gently, and then more vigorously, push me out of the way, I waver, almost falling several feet into a cart selling flowers below. The incense engulfs me in pine-scented smoke and I'm suddenly afraid I'm going to faint or fall or stumble on the narrow step. So much stimulation by sound, color, scent and movement disrupts my equilibrium, and I lurch and lose balance like I'm drunk. A young man dressed in the wild colors of the Mayan *indios* grabs my arms to keep me from falling into the mayhem below. He doesn't let go and steadies my wavering stance. We stand there for a few seconds while *bombas* explode close to our feet. I can feel the flash of heat from the fiery detonations.

Acting like a crazy old lady caught in a centuries-old time warp, I hold onto the young man until I regain my equilibrium. The smoke clears, the *bombas* cease their continuous eruptions, and I release my grip on my rescuer, the man in the Mayan costume. He looks me in the eye, smiles, and quietly backs away. "*Gracias,*" I murmur, wishing I could tell him more. I feel like I've been touched by a holy man.

The *cofradias* carry the platforms of Jesus and the saints into the church, the procession ends, and the marketplace is once again a bustle of commerce and trade. My ears ringing from the *bombas,* I gingerly make my way down the steps of the church. Feeling both embarrassed and hallucinatory, as in a dream, a part of me floats to the bottom of the stairs. All is well.

I join Judy below and we begin to do some serious shopping. Hugging my shoulder bag to my body, watching carefully for possible pickpocket thieves, I begin browsing the narrow aisles of brilliant handwoven textiles, straw hats, wooden masks, and traditional *huipiles.* The slap-slap of women patting cornmeal into thick tortillas lends a soft cadence to the bustle of the market. I buy a few of these warm, fresh tortillas and munch on one while perusing the wares.

Suddenly a surge of people crowds the aisle, mostly indigenous Mayan women in traditional dress, many with babies wrapped in colorful *rebozos* clinging to their backs. They're pushing ahead, and I'm literally lifted off my feet for a moment as they surge around me, in back of me, in front of me. I feel panic as my feet leave the ground. Judy is twenty or more feet ahead, and the crowd sweeps around her as well. I clutch my purse tightly and just let the surging, pushing throng lift me. The cluster of people passes through like a blast of wind. It's a small tornado of frenzy and movement, and then calm prevails.

Judy and I laugh, bewildered and surprised by the hurricane of people. Realizing that we're obvious tourists, I'm now conscious that we're targets. We have money, while so many people around us have none. I check my purse and pockets and find that my money and passport are intact. We shop, we buy, we eat a delicious lunch of tortillas and grilled chicken roasted on an open fire, and we sit on a curb and watch the parade of vendors hawking their goods. It is a day to remember.

Several hours later, tucked away in our hotel in another city, we sip wine on our garden balcony and watch the sun set. Judy rummages through her cargo pants and backpack.

"Have you seen my passport?"

"Nope. Did you check the drawers and bureaus in the room?"

Twenty minutes of searching ensues, and Judy empties her backpack on the bed. Her wallet is intact and her money is accounted for. But there is no passport.

We recall the encounter with the hurricane surge of people at the market in Chichi. The pressing of people physically walking directionally against us, the confusion and excitement of the busy marketplace, and our focus on the goods displayed in the venues must have diverted our attention. We were on a mission to make deals and buy the textiles and purses and blouses. I was snapping photographs, trying to capture the color and the faces of Guatemala, while Judy was bargaining up and down the aisles.

We were absorbed in our shopping. Our guard was down.

As we let the implications of this assault on our personal property sink in, we sit on our treasured balcony contemplating what we should do. Neither of us sleeps well that night. Judy needs that passport to return home. That's a given. This means shortening our time exploring Guatemala and heading back to the U.S. Embassy in Guatemala City. Dealing with the bureaucracy of the U.S. government is not part of our vacation plan, but we're at the end of our time in Guatemala, and we don't know how long it will take to replace a lost passport. Hours? Days?

We decide to leave the next day for Guatemala City and begin the process.

My phone buzzes with a text message. It is J.C. He wants to know where we are and will drive to our hotel for one last visit. I text him back and tell him that we have to replace a lost passport and are returning to Guatemala City.

I add: "It is not possible for you to visit me in Guatemala City. I will talk to you when I return to the U.S.A."

TWENTY-EIGHT

Portrait of a President

Margarita

IN GUATEMALA CITY, we go to the U.S. Embassy at 7 a.m. the next day and are the first in line when the office opens an hour later. The building is simple, blocky and utilitarian, in many shades of gray. If you lived here for decades, you'd probably never notice that the building existed. It disappears into the drab neutrals of urban architecture.

There are long lines outside the main entrance where people are waiting, hoping for visas and passports. We're directed to a special room for American citizens and are the first ones to enter. Rows of orange plastic chairs and a wall of glass windows line one side of the empty room. Judy immediately notices that there is no photograph of President Obama in the room, and she mentions this to me. She is annoyed with this diplomatic slight and mutters something about the general incompetence of embassies in Latin America.

When an embassy officer enters the room, she asks about this. "Where are the pictures of President Obama and Vice President Biden?"

The officer looks at her perplexed.

"This is the U.S. Embassy, correct? I am in the place for a lost passport, correct?" Her tone has an edge to it, noticeable from across the room. Judy is not subtle.

"Yes, this is the U.S. Embassy," the officer replies.

"They why aren't you displaying a photograph of the president of the United States?"

The officer shrugs. He doesn't have an answer.

Sister Judy, who spent twelve years in Guatemala during the civil wars of the 1980s and '90s, has no patience with the bureaucracy and politics of the U.S. government. She is assertive, to the point of being mildly and pointedly aggressive with the agents behind the glass windows. Heretofore unfailingly polite, she has a sharp inflection in her voice today. She remembers the deception of American policy during those years. She remembers the killings, the assassinations, the fear and the oppression of the Guatemalan people. She remembers the lies. Knowing that the U.S. government was surreptitiously involved in supplying arms, money and training to the Guatemalan military, she's uncomfortable dealing with the embassy. Why should she trust these people now? She's ready to take them on.

Privately, I worry that she'll never get her stolen passport replaced if this is the tenor of conversation. Sometimes you just have to play the game if you want to get your business done.

Judy, however, is relentless.

When called to the window to state her business, the bureaucrat speaks Spanish as he instructs her how to proceed. Judy, who speaks fluent Spanish, is visibly annoyed. She repeats a question: "This is the U.S. Embassy, correct?"

"Yes," the agent behind the glass says.

"Then why are you speaking Spanish to me? I am a U.S. citizen, and I want to know why you are not speaking English to me."

The agent is visibly flustered.

The conversation continues, both in Spanish and English, and the tension between them crackles. The agent asks her in Spanish to fill out a form on a computer sitting in the corner of the room. The computer is probably fifteen years old. Judy refuses. She figures that the computer will undoubtedly freeze up, develop a glitch, and she will then be relegated to the end of the line. We'll never get out of here. It's a typical stalling tactic. A transaction that should take thirty minutes will now take six hours. Possibly more.

She asks for a paper copy and will fill out the form by hand rather than struggling with the ancient computer. The agent tells her there is no paper copy. Judy bristles. "I want to speak with your manager," she says in English.

The agent leaves the window shaking his head, not quite knowing how to proceed. The room behind the glass is filled with at least ten metal desks, and the office is bustling with officious-looking people. There is no color in the room and shades of gun-metal gray prevail. After several minutes, a middle-aged American white man with thinning hair comes to the window and politely asks if he can be of help. I notice he has on a red tie with an American flag tie clip. It's the only spot of color in the room. For some reason, his red tie gives me hope.

"I would like a paper copy of the forms for a lost passport," Judy says. "I would like the agents to speak English first during this transaction because this is the room for Americans who have passport issues. And lastly, where is the photograph of President Obama?"

The agent, probably the office manager, has kind eyes and a friendly smile. "The official portrait of President Obama is in the main foyer," he says. "You probably missed it when you entered the building."

He busies himself behind a computer screen and then accesses Judy's contact information. "So you live in Douglas, Arizona?" he adds, smiling behind his bifocals.

"Yes, I do."

"Well, my home is in Portal, Arizona, close to your home. What brings you to Guatemala, and how did you lose your passport?"

For the next twenty minutes, Judy and the agent swap stories of the Chiricahua Mountains, the desert in spring, and favorite camping places. The tension melts, and there's laughter and private jokes about the local politics of Arizona.

Judy has her passport within two hours.

I slip out of the room during all this business to look for that portrait of President Obama. And there it is, along with Vice President Biden. The photos are small, maybe eight by ten inches, enclosed in a simple wooden frame. I have to search the room for them. They hang in a dark corner of the main lobby. I guess I expected something larger and more prominent in a U.S. Embassy in a foreign country—a portrait with a gold frame and a prominent American flag gracing the entry-way.

I'm suddenly self-consciously aware than I have no idea who the president of Guatemala is.

After leaving the embassy, we have a delicious lunch in downtown Guatemala City, and we're on a plane home within two days. We stumble through security check-points at the airport. Judy is detained several times because her new passport is not registered on any computer system. Thanks to the computer glitch, we miss a 9 p.m. connecting flight home from Houston. So we collapse in an airport lounge, order two glasses of wine, and laugh about it all. We dine on Vietnamese lettuce wraps, and I decide that this is the best airport food I've ever had. We order two more glasses of wine and raise a toast to our adventure.

Arriving back in Tucson well after midnight, we're both giddy and exhausted from the wine, the lengthy flight, and the relief to be once again in our beloved desert. We are home.

TWENTY-NINE

———⟹ • ⟸———

La Tienda (The Store)

Margarita

DURING THE SUMMER of 2015, I settle back into life in southern Arizona. There are weekly trips to *el comedor*, in Nogales, Sonora. I continue volunteering with the Green Valley/Sahuarita Samaritans every week, serving breakfast and distributing clothes and conversation to the weary and tattered. It is simple, it is direct, and it is complicated all at once. The needs of the people are enormous, and they keep coming and coming, seeking a better life. The promised land.

Each time I wear one of the colorful blouses from Guatemala, I think about Juan Carlos, wondering how he is faring. Mailing packages to his family is a chancy endeavor, but I send some photos and clothes for his children to his rural village. He never receives the package. J.C. has access to a computer only when he travels to a larger town, and his trips are sporadic, so my emails go unanswered. Phone calls are the best way to communicate, but the reception is often poor and the crackles and disconnections come often.

A few weeks after my return, Juan Carlos begins calling our home. He works some days on the mountainside cultivating coffee plants. Other days he drives a school bus. There are times when I get an email while he is in Xela and I envision him sitting in an Internet café. One evening he calls to tell me that Maria is pregnant. He sounds both happy and worried. The baby is due in December.

Another time he emails me photos of a small house made of concrete block. Graffiti fills the outside walls of the small shack, and it looks abandoned and run-down. He wants to buy this house, and asks me if I can help him with a down payment. The owner is asking ten thousand dollars, American dollars. The shack isn't worth one thousand dollars, in my opinion, but J.C. is desperate to move out of his parents' home.

"No, I can't help you with such a large and important purchase," I tell him. Feeling like a stern parent, I draw some boundaries. I explain that I can manage to send small amounts of money every month, but ten thousand dollars is too much.

I ponder Juan Carlos's options. He did have a simple business plan during my visit to his home and had figured that about five thousand dollars would cover start-up costs for a small *tienda* in his village. He would sell staples, soft drinks, maybe some fresh fruit and vegetables from the front porch of his home.

After a few weeks of thought and discussion with my husband, I call J.C. and tell him I could send him a lump sum of two thousand dollars and would also send a few hundred dollars each month.

"Will this help you set up a small *tienda*?"

Ecstatic, J.C. calls me the following night just to make sure he understood our phone conversation. "Gracias a Dios," (thank God) is peppered throughout our conversation.

"I want to help with the expenses of the new baby, and also I want you to develop your own store in your village," I suggest. Once I send the money, I must let go of any control.

It's Juan Carlos's life, not mine. If he spends the money on a car or new clothes or a freezer full of food, it's out of my hands. This is not a

loan; this is a gift to a family struggling to make a life in an impover-
ished village in a country plagued with political upheaval. Bottom line:
I don't want Juan Carlos to migrate to the United States. His growing
family needs him in Guatemala.

———— • ————

SENDING TWO THOUSAND dollars to Guatemala via Western
Union is fraught with complications. I fill out the necessary forms for
the transaction, and the officious agent at the Western Union window
admonishes me for trying to send such a large amount.

"I'm sorry, but Western Union never accepts such a large amount
of cash. Do you know the person who will be receiving this money?"

I'm taken aback by this response. Five people are standing behind
me in line, impatient to purchase their lottery ticket or a carton of cigarettes from a stack locked up in a case.

"Why can't I send two thousand dollars?"

"It's policy."

"So, what's the policy? Is there a limit on money you can send to
Guatemala? And I can send this money to whomever I wish, right? I
mean, it's my money."

The Western Union woman looks me over. "One moment, please."

The people behind me groan. A couple of them leave in a huff.

Western Union woman returns to the window. "The maximum
amount you can send is five hundred dollars at one time." She looks
me in the eye. "Is this person in Guatemala a family member?"

"No, he's a good friend. And why do you ask?"

"It's policy. Have you ever met this person face-to-face?"

I can't believe this affront to my privacy. Does Western Union believe
that large amounts of money are most likely drug transactions, espe-

cially if it involves a Latin American country? And does this woman really have the right to question to whom I am sending this money?

Okay. Great. I live about an hour from the Western Union office, which means I'll spend eight hours making the round trip four times to send two thousand dollars. I am annoyed with the system.

At this point, resolving the money transfer issue is my primary goal. I fill out more forms with the amount of five hundred dollars, and the agent completes the paper-work. She isn't happy with my questions. The people in the long line behind me aren't happy. And I'm not happy. But we get it done.

Later that night I call J.C. and explain that I'll be sending him money over the next four days in batches of five hundred dollars. He's flabbergasted. Four times he asks me if he is understanding my words correctly.

"Two thousand dollars, *americano*, Margarita? Two thousand? *No palabras.*" No words.

"I want you to open your *tienda* and send me photos of your progress with this business dream."

In a few weeks I get an email photo of Juan Carlos and two cows, with his little daughter hanging on the neck of a small calf. She's wearing rubber flip-flop sandals, and her toes are covered in mud and manure. There's a smear of mud on her nose. Staring at the photo, I have trouble comprehending what this is all about. He looks proud and happy, standing by one of the cows. His daughter is clearly in love with the calf. Even the calf is smiling. It is an endearing photo which I look at frequently.

Then I get it. J.C. is going to fatten up these cows and sell the meat. He'll create a *carnicería* in his village. There are no meat markets in any of the nearby towns in these coastal mountains, and he will sell beef to customers eager to buy some home-grown protein.

Juan Carlos calls me, and sounds absolutely elated about the windfall of funds. He puts his wife on the phone, and she speaks rapidly, with many *"gracias a dios"* interspersed in the conversation. I understand about one-third of the words and do my best to keep up.

Later, I continue my exchange with J.C. and ask, "So what about the small *tienda* with fresh vegetables and fruits and staples?"

"This is better. No one sells meat in these villages. It will be my new work. But first I must fatten up the cows."

It's time for me to let it go. Let J.C. take control of his entrepreneurial dream. Get out of the way. Forget about the fruits and vegetables. He'll have a meat market in the highlands of Guatemala, the only *carnicería* for miles. I would love to be there, petting the calf and watching the children help with the chores. I hope they don't get too attached to the calf.

I light a candle in my home that evening for hope and fat cattle.

THIRTY

New Life

Margarita

RAISING A FAMILY when there is never enough money is a recurring theme in most corners of the world. Juan Carlos calls frequently with the monetary crisis of the day. The truck breaks down so he can't deliver his packages of fresh beef to neighboring villages. Maria has a difficult pregnancy and is hospitalized for dehydration. Juanito, now age six, has appendicitis and is rushed to the hospital. Maria's mother dies, and the funeral expenses are enormous.

One night, J.C. calls in a panic. It's early December and Maria is in the hospital. J.C.'s voice has an edge of hysteria. His Spanish is rapid-fire.

"Maria is working for so long all night," he tells me.

"Maria is working? Why is she working at night?"

"No, no, no. She is having the pains of the working. *Como se dice...* She is having the pains of the labor. She is working hard for many hours. The baby is coming!"

"Ah! Maria is in labor! *Ahora entiendo.* Now I understand."

They are in a birthing hospital somewhere, and I can hear rattling metal pans, footsteps, and activity in the background.

"They will not give her medicine for the pain. She is screaming. It is a clinic for poor people. I do not have the money for the big hospital. If I had more money, they would give her the pain medicine."

Quietly I consider this. It's probably better for the baby if Maria doesn't have pain medicine. She's had two children. She knows the drill. Juan Carlos probably needs pain medicine more than his wife, who is hunkering down and pushing their baby out into the world.

Feeling helpless and clueless about what's really going on, I let Juan Carlos talk about whatever he wishes. We talk about his *carnicería* and the intricacies involved in raising cows, butchering the animals, packaging the meat in a sanitary manner, and then burying the beef in ice in the back of his pickup truck and delivering it to the surrounding villages.

"I do not sleep for three days. We start on Thursday and stay up all night butchering the cow. Then we package the meat on Friday, and I can only stay awake with many cups of coffee. Saturday I drive all day to restaurants and markets selling the meat. More and more people are buying my beef. When I finish my deliveries, we go to church on Saturday night."

Chuckling, I tell him he'll probably be staying up many more nights with a new baby.

"I am so happy with my new life and my new work. But I need Maria to help me, and now she is here having this baby. Plus, living with my parents is hard. We are crowded, and now there will be one more person in the house."

J.C. vents and whines for a while.

"But your life is better now in Guatemala, *es verdad?*"

In the United States he would be living in the shadows, waiting for *la migra* to appear unexpectedly and take him to a prison or deport him back to Guatemala. We agree that it's difficult to make enough money to support a family no matter where you are.

"Yes, Margarita, it is better to be in Guatemala now."

Our conversation is intimate and emotional, and I'm surprised that he's called me at this exceptional moment in the life of his family. His voice wavers and stumbles. He is on the edge of tears. I hear commotion in the background—a dog barking, a siren wailing, the static of our poor phone connection, voices in a hallway. I wish I were there with both of them, helping Maria breathe through labor and supporting both of them as this baby makes its way into the world.

"Juan Carlos, I want you to go and be with Maria and help her take deep breaths during contractions. She needs you beside her."

He hangs up and I think about Maria all night. The next day J.C. calls me to announce the birth of his new daughter, Leila. Photos appear on my email stream, and Maria smiles weakly into the camera, holding a newborn infant with a thick head of black hair. J.C. is elated about this new addition to his family life. I feel like a godparent.

In three weeks I receive more photos of cows, calves, a baby, and Maria. Baby Leila is wrapped in a *rebozo* on Maria's back while she weighs hunks of meat on a hanging scale. There is blood everywhere, smeared on her apron, smeared on her cheek. It looks like a scene out of a Quentin Tarantino movie. Maria flashes a huge grin as she raises a chunk of beef liver in one hand and a bloody knife in the other. She has wasted no time getting back into the tasks of the day, weighing and packaging meat so Juan Carlos can deliver the product. Little Leila's head peeps just above the *rebozo*. It is the most bizarre photo of a mother and child I've ever seen.

Months pass. Our phone calls are punctuated with baby cries, barking dogs, and the crackling of our phone connection. We disconnect frequently. I call back, J.C. calls back, and we take turns trying to complete our conversation before the phone fizzles out.

There's baby colic, Maria's breast infection, and a major truck breakdown that means the meat can't be delivered. The rhythm of life is fragile. One week the baby is gaining weight; the next week the baby loses weight. Someone in the family always has *el gripe*, the flu.

When Juan Carlos's mother becomes seriously ill, there are many phone calls. J.C. is despairing. He can't afford all the medicine for his mother, who is now staying in Xela with one of Juan Carlos's sisters. Xela is the nearest large city, and is a three hour drive from J.C.'s village.

His mother is probably in her early fifties. She has a classic Mayan face and has lived through the tumultuous years of political upheaval in Guatemala. I can't discern exactly what's wrong with Alicia. He speaks of "black urine" and her lack of appetite. He can't bear to be with her because she is having so much pain *en el estomago* (in the stomach). Once again I let him talk, half in Spanish, half in English.

"I am broken, Margarita."

Picturing him rocking back and forth in despair sitting outside on the curb in front of his house, all I can do is listen. The phone hisses. I miss sentences as I strain to understand through the static.

"I am broken into pieces, Margarita."

There are long silences on the phone. I don't have the words, in either English or Spanish, to support him. Silence and time are all I have.

Although he doesn't ask, I send extra money when I can for the baby, for the grandmother, for truck repairs. Doggedly, J.C. keeps pushing on, doing his best to keep the family afloat. Most of the time he succeeds.

I love the phone calls when he is high on his successes. The cows are fat, the kids aren't sick, Maria is helping with the family business, and the truck can make it over the mountain roads.

⸺⸺ • ⸺⸺

ONE DAY IN mid-December 2016, Juan Carlos calls to tell me that his nephew, Roberto, is missing somewhere in the desert near Laredo, Texas. Roberto is trying to get to a city in the United States to work and send money home. This is his first attempt to cross into the United States, and his family has not heard from him for three days. Roberto has a cell phone, and the battery is probably dead.

"Can you drive to Laredo and look for Roberto, Margarita?"

"Laredo? Laredo, Texas? That's a two-day drive from our ranch, Juan Carlos. Maybe three days. Texas is a big state. The desert is huge. I wouldn't know where to look."

Two hours later J.C. sends me photos of his nephew and a Google map of the Texas borderlands. I stare at the pictures. Roberto looks like a typical high school teenager, possibly seventeen. His hair is neatly combed and he sports a pair of stylish horn-rimmed glasses. I study several Google maps and the little orange balloon marker indicating where Roberto was when he last made contact.

I have a friend who works with the Colibri Center for Human Rights, an organization in Tucson that identifies the names of human remains found in the desert and then contacts families. Emailing her immediately, I send her the photos and maps. She puts me in touch with a search and rescue organization in Texas and gives me the phone number of a colleague in the Laredo area. I call Juan Carlos with this information, and instruct him to call the person in Texas.

J.C. is wary. "Is this person with *la migra*?"

I assure him that the rescue team is not affiliated with Homeland Security. Privately I'm struck by J.C.'s distrust of the Border Patrol and Homeland Security, given the fact that his nephew needs rescuing within the next few days or he may die in the Texas desert. It seems to me that the more agencies that search for Roberto, the better the chances that the young man will be found alive. And Juan Carlos wants his nephew found, to be sure. But he doesn't want him to languish in a prison for months. J.C. can't erase the prison memories from his own mind.

In two days there is good news. Roberto has been found and he's doing well. A few weeks later, Juan Carlos calls to tell me that a Mexican-American family in Texas has taken Roberto into their home and nursed him back to health. He goes on to stay with the family for two weeks, and arrangements are made for a ride to another state. Ultimately, Roberto reunites with some family members in the Midwest and gets a job in construction. All of this is done under the radar, and the federal government is not a part of the rescue.

I'm so happy about this ending but can't help thinking that if I'd been more resourceful and maybe more gutsy, I could have gotten J.C. to a safe place in the U.S. But, of course, he wouldn't be with his own family in Guatemala, wouldn't have a business he is trying to keep solvent, and wouldn't have a new baby girl, Leila.

There are trade-offs no matter what path we choose.

THIRTY-ONE

A Crisis

Margarita

WHAT HAPPENED TO Juan Carlos is not unusual—that is, fleeing from a violent, corrupt country where he was threatened with a gun to his head and extorted for large sums of money. He was lost in the Arizona desert, rescued by a couple of clueless citizens (my husband and me) who did their best to help, picked up by Border Patrol agents after walking for three days to the outskirts of Tucson, and summarily taken to a detention center. This happens every day in the land that claims to care about the huddled masses yearning to be free. Most of us don't ever have to think about this in any meaningful way, but if you live in the Arizona desert and pay attention, you do think about these things. It's the only way to remain human.

Our immigration system is reprehensible and indescribably cruel, and yet it's easy to ignore. Juan Carlos was locked up for months and coerced into submission. He was told it would be a lengthy incarceration, possibly years, before his case would be processed. He was encouraged to return to Guatemala in spite of the risks to his life that he faced when he went to work every day driving a bus.

Because this was Juan Carlos's third illegal crossing into the U.S., (he'd spent time in a detention center twice) and there were records of his capture, he wasn't a good candidate for asylum. Entering the asylum process is a basic human right and one that most Americans believe is a part of our national heritage. The United Nations established a protocol in 1951 outlining this criterion: A person qualifies for asylum when they can prove a well-documented fear of persecution in their home country based on race, religion, nationality, social group, or political opinion. Applicants must show that they are targeted for one of the reasons listed and that the country where they live is unable to protect them.

Juan Carlos had letters from his employer, neighbors, and friends in Guatemala explicitly describing the dangers he faced every time he went to work. This was not enough. He was damned by his circumstances and became yet another punching bag for the politicos who seek easy answers.

Three letters from employers in Guatemala were left for me to keep in case he applies for asylum in the future. One of them reads as follows:

MUNICIPALITY OF THE VILLAGE OF COLOMBA

The undersigned Municipal Mayor of the Village of Colomba Costa Cuca, Department of Quetzaltenango presently states:
   That Mr. Juan Carlos xxxxxxxx who is identified by the personal document of identification No. CUI: xxxx drawn up by the National Registry of People of the Republic of Guatemala, with residency in the Agrarian Community xxxxx in the municipality of xxxxx is a person I have known previously. He is a responsible person, he is respectful and hardworking, but due to the crime wave that is prevalent in the country and to safeguard his physical safety he had to emigrate to the U.S.A, because he

has been constantly threatened by antisocial groups that threat-
ened to eliminate him physically if he didn't give them a certain
quantity of money. For this reason he had to make the above
mentioned decision.

   In response to the request of the interested party I extend, seal,
and sign the present document on letterhead stationary of this
municipality etc. on the 17th day of March, 2014.

All the employers' letters state that J.C. was risking his life every time he went to work, but the letters were not enough to speed up the asylum process for my friend.

These realities about asylum and immigration policy are not simplistic, liberal railings against the present administration of President Donald Trump in 2017. Let us not forget that the Obama administration deported more than three million migrants, sending them asunder all over the world. I have witnessed first-hand what this does to families who have been separated, and I have watched young men and women weep every week at the Nogales aid station where I volunteer. Their crime is crossing a border without the proper papers. The crucial documentation is next to impossible to obtain because the United States has no coherent policy regarding the migration of desperate people.

It is difficult to forgive our government for this dysfunctional and utterly diabolical system, especially when American trade policies like the North American Free Trade Agreement, (NAFTA) and the Central American Free Trade Agreement, (CAFTA) have contributed to the collapse of farms and an agrarian culture. People who were once able to support their families in rural Guatemala and Mexico have been forced out of business. NAFTA and CAFTA have contributed to the collapse of small family farms, and hundreds of thousands of people have migrated to greener pastures. Add to this the profound climate changes throughout the world that have millions of people on the move.

And then there's the lucrative drug corridor that connects the United States with a large swath of Latin America. Huge sums of money are passed back and forth because of the enormous consumption of illicit drugs in this country. Business is business, and the human toll is incalculable on both sides of the border.

THIRTY-TWO

Entrepreneur

Margarita

FIVE YEARS HAVE passed since Juan Carlos, in his flapping black garbage bag *serape,* called to me from across the canyon. "Help me, help me, I am lost. My heart, it is dying."

Today he is working hard to develop his own business, a *carnicería* in the western highlands of Guatemala. His family is growing, and the third child, Leila, is thriving. A fourth infant was born two weeks ago. The two older children, Lupita and Juanito, attend school in the small village where they've lived all of their lives. Lupita is seven years old and Juanito is nine. The family is poor, but there's money coming in every week from the meat business. Juan Carlos still lives in a house with his parents, siblings, and their mates and children. He isn't happy with this arrangement, and is constantly trying to figure out how to move into a house of his own.

Every phone call I get from Juan Carlos includes this question: When are you coming back? As much as I would love to return to Guatemala, I'm not as hardy as I was a few years ago. The journey had its ups and downs. Long hours in a bus, a shuttle, and a pickup truck. Bumpy roads. Lack of sleep and low energy on some days, high energy on others.

My encounter with Juan Carlos was a direct meeting of the rich and the poor. J.C. was the poorest and most desperate man I've ever welcomed into our home. He thinks about money and the basic elements of life—food, clothing, shelter, education for his children—every day. My husband and I, by contrast, are moderately financially secure and don't worry about money. That said, I don't have money to travel extensively.

I learned many things from my encounter with J.C.. When he landed on our doorstep, he was as vulnerable as any person could possibly be. He was exhausted, starving, and mentally confused. We spoke different languages. We were strangers. He was wearing rags, was caked in dirt and mud, and was reduced to drinking his own urine. He was afraid he would be shot and thrown in a ditch.

And yet he carried himself with great dignity. He opened his heart and spirit to Lester and me at this very low point in his life. He looked me in the eye and said, "Help me." His only option was to trust that we would help him. And we did. I think most people would do the same thing. We're not exceptional. We did the best we could.

Juan Carlos brought up many feelings in me, and I'm not proud of some of them. When he landed on our patio, I was initially afraid of his fragile condition. I wanted to take him to a hospital. I felt incompetent in dealing with his physical and psychological frailty. I was also terrified of being caught by *la migra*. Harboring an undocumented person in Arizona is a federal offense.

Suddenly I was suspicious of my neighbors, fearing they would call Homeland Security. If someone had dropped in unexpectedly during the days before Christmas, Immigration and Customs Enforcement (ICE) might later have come knocking on my door.

And it was Christmas week and I had a long list of things to do: baking, shopping, dinners with friends, hosting guests at our ranch, a tree to decorate, concerts to attend. Here I was with a stranger, the "other," obliterating my best laid plans. I selfishly wanted to stick to my holiday to-do list.

He shook up my world. I thank him for that.

Even now, years later, when he calls, I'm never quite sure why he wants to talk. Our conversations are simple.

"*Hola,* Margarita. How are you? How is your *esposo?* What are you doing this minute?"

We talk about our lives, our health, the weather, his children, the *carnicería* business. I hear about the teething, the colic, the school, and often about the fatigue he experiences when preparing the meat for the next days of butchering and delivery. It's taken me a while to realize that J.C. isn't calling me because he's in a crisis or needs money. I believe it shames him to be in need.

He wants to talk because he likes sharing the day-to-day events of his life. I'm the curious, offbeat *americana* lady who lives up north and helped him out when he was half-crazed with hunger and fear.

WHILE CHOPPING VEGETABLES and whipping up eggs for a supper *frittata,* the phone rings, and after a long pause with a lot of noisy static and crackles, Juan Carlos greets me.

"Hola, Margarita."

He chuckles, and I immediately know he is in a teasing mood and this isn't a crisis call. After putting down my knife, I sit out on the patio and do my best to discern the scattered English and Spanish words that come pouring over the line.

We go through the usual formalities: "How are you? How is your *esposo?* What are you doing this moment? God bless you for your help with my family."

Then his voice rises excitedly and he tells me the real reason for the call.

"I am driving into the city tomorrow to purchase a freezer for my *carnicería.* With the money from my business and your help, I can buy a new freezer and deliver the meat to all of the customers without all the ice piled in my truck."

This is indeed wonderful news. A relief, actually. Sometimes I worried about how he was safely delivering meat to distant villages in his pickup truck. Guatemala is a tropical country, ice melts quickly, and delivering spoiled meat is bad for business, not to mention dangerous to the consumer. A freezer will ameliorate this problem. He can freeze the meat and deliver the product safely.

Two days later he emails me a photo of his children with their arms around a freezer. Instead of hugging a baby calf, they're hugging a freezer.

Juan Carlos is beside himself with joy about all of this. He puts Lupita on the line and she chatters about helping her daddy package the meat. Lupita is in the second grade at her primary school. She calls me *abuelita Margarita.* I love it.

Maria also speaks to me, and I can hear baby Leila's squeaks and shrieks in the background. She tells me Juanito is now quite a soccer player, and J.C. plans to buy him the proper shoes and uniform for the *fútbol.* The parrot, the television, the baby, and the friendly chaos of a house full of children are all a delightful symphony of vibrant life.

"We will go to one of the big stores to get these things. I am so happy!" J.C. is exuberant about this week of good fortune. True, he is working two jobs—driving a school bus in addition to developing his *carnicería* business. Also true, he has been coughing for weeks with *el gripe,* but seems better.

The entrepreneurial spirit of my Guatemalan friend is full of American ingenuity and tenacity, and I'm delighted to have been a small part of it all. Finishing our supper that evening, Lester and I toast our Guatemalan friend—the "other." I wish I'd had some of Juan Carlos's flank steak to add to this meal. And his fresh eggs.

THIRTY-THREE

Repercussions

Margarita

MY COUNTRY HAS a new president, Donald Trump, a man who put his cards on the table during his first campaign speech on June 16, 2015. His words created a firestorm in the Latino community and among the people of the borderlands.

Those words are still ringing in my ears:

> *"When Mexico sends its people, they're not sending their best. They're not sending you. They're not sending you. They're sending people that have lots of problems, and they're bringing those problems with us. They're bringing drugs. They're bringing crimes. They're rapists."*

The overt racism of Trump's first speech announcing his candidacy astounds me today, more than a year after the people of my country elected him. These were the first words out of his mouth. I didn't think he had a chance during those first months. I couldn't have been more misguided.

In the most surprising presidential election upset of my lifetime, a racist, misogynist bully who was a reality TV performer and real estate mogul—this man who hates Mexicans and Central Americans—was elected the forty-fifth president of the United States. In the weeks before his January 20 inauguration, I was in a state of agitation and disbelief.

Driving eighty miles to Tucson on a rainy, blustery day, January 21, 2017, was the best decision I made for myself during my post-election fog. I decided to join the Women's March in Tucson, marching in solidarity with women in Washington, D.C. Thousands were gathering in a small park in downtown Tucson. A sea of "pink pussy caps" and handmade signs filled the streets and alleyways as we walked to the starting point of the parade. The pink knitted caps were a disavowal of Trump's crude remarks about grabbing women's crotches whenever he felt like it, remarks that surfaced during his campaign. I waved to a few Tucson city police officers wearing the pink caps. Scheduling the Women's March for the day after Trump's inauguration was a brilliant tactical move. It felt like the whole world was celebrating the issues of women, but also repudiating the vileness of Trump's message.

I marched in Tucson with more than fifteen thousand others—women, men, children, dogs—amid a sea of clever signs expressing the fears and hopes of the next four years. The march took place in every major city in the country and spread across seven continents. It was the largest demonstration in the history of the United States and possibly the largest outpouring of sentiment throughout the world. Millions of men, women and children hit the streets.

Parading alongside my brothers and sisters, I felt a connection and solidarity with the politics of humanity. I saw strangers helping people in wheelchairs as they joined the thousands in the street. People shared food and, during the sporadic rain showers, umbrellas. Fathers lifted their children high on their shoulders so they could see the mass of diversity pouring into the Tucson streets.

Photos and emails shot through cyberspace from everywhere, both in this country and throughout the world. I saw crowds marching through the streets of Paris and hundreds proudly hiking along a dusty road in Nigeria. These images continued streaming on my cell phone for days. My friend Julie flew to Washington and sent photos of women in pink pussy hats squished together on the Metro. Her messages were euphoric, and weeks later she was still energized, exalting in the love and connection she felt in the streets of D.C. The reports throughout the world proclaimed "Build bridges, not walls." A banner hung from a crane near the White House with one word: "Resist!"

And yet in spite of this image of solidarity, I cannot think of a time when the country has been more polarized. The dark underbelly of the United States has emerged in a hundred ways. Muslim mosques have been destroyed by fire in American cities; immigrants and even tourists with proper documentation are being detained at airports; Jewish cemeteries are being desecrated. ICE agents are knocking on doors in the early morning hours or showing up at middle schools as parents pick up their children, capturing people who may or may not have the proper documentation to legally live in this country. Families are ripped apart without warning. There is a palpable fear in every city in the United States where immigrants reside.

I talk with undocumented people at *el comedor* who have lived in the U.S. for decades, committed no crime (except the crime of not having proper papers), and have families and good jobs. Suddenly they are deported to Nogales, Sonora, where they have no ties. Often Homeland Security agents have confiscated their money and identification. They are in shock, trying their best to figure out how to return to their homes in the United States.

On one of my visits to *el comedor,* I met a man of about thirty years who was taller than many of the migrants, spoke Spanish with a Bronx accent, and looked well-nourished. He had just been released from thirty days in a detention center in Eloy, Arizona, and his wallet, cell phone, clothes and identification had been "lost" somewhere along the way, probably during his incarceration. He was from New York and arrived in the U.S. when he was six months old. His primary language was English, but he was also fluent in Spanish. Educated in American public schools, he was attending a community college and studying to be a chef. Acting as a sous-chef at an upscale restaurant in New York City, he was picked up late at night by ICE at his workplace. He had never heard of the city of Nogales, so we showed him where he was on a tattered map taped to the wall.

His confusion and disorientation were conspicuous. Barely holding himself together, his life was in upheaval. He knew no one in Nogales; his friends and family were thousands of miles away.

The Samaritans stepped up and connected him with resources at *el comedor*. He called his family, arranged for some money to be wired to Nogales, and made a decision to travel to Puebla, where he had relatives he'd never met. We passed the hat and collected money for a bus ticket.

"I've never broken the law. Not even a speeding ticket."

I feel certain that this man will make it, either in Mexico or in the U.S. He is bilingual, he has a marketable skill, he is educated, and he is young and strong. But what a waste of human potential, and what a disruption to his life.

During the turbulent days of Trump's first two years in the White House, I'm relieved that Juan Carlos is creating a life in a remote village of Guatemala. He buys a few cows and calves, raises them, butchers the meat, and sells the product to surrounding villages. Some months there are profits to celebrate, and other months there are more bills than he can manage. The normal crises of family life, with sick children, an ailing mother, and a crowded home of three generations, cause my friend a lot of stress.

Juan Carlos calls me frequently, and he's like another member of my family who is checking in, catching me up on the latest news from his mountain home. Truth be told, J.C. calls me more than my own children do. Mostly I listen, and we often end our conversations chuckling about the twists and turns of our lives. I've had long conversations with Lupita, and barely follow as she chatters on about her school, her brother, her dolls. Her Spanish is rapid and staccato, and I catch every fourth word, trying my best to string them all together.

Reflecting on my adventure with Juan Carlos, I can't forget that I am a white American woman well into her seventh decade. In spite of my distaste for the new guy in the White House as of 2017, I don't fear a scarcity of food on the dinner table, or fret about paying the bills each month. I'm not in survival mode as so many others are.

For people of a certain age, there is a notion that now is the time to dial it down and limit our risks. On the contrary, I believe we should be raising hell, directing our energies toward the things we care about. Playing it safe is a cop-out. Especially when we may not have many years left.

The other day I took a group of young men to the Nogales border to view the wall. They had grown up in Brownsville, Texas, which is also along the border, but now live in Indiana and Minnesota. Their journey along the entire border wall—all seven hundred miles of it—extended from Brownsville to Tijuana, and they documented the experience with photos and videos. They wanted to talk to some migrants and learn about aspects of border life from local residents and activists. We had a great day together, with some serendipitous interviews along the streets of Nogales, Sonora.

As we said our good-byes at the end of the day, one of them said to me, "Please be careful." It was not a casual passing remark. He looked me in the eye, and with all the conviction of his twenty-three-year-old self, he squeezed my hand and really meant it.

Be careful.

His words took me by surprise and have stayed with me for days. My perception of my own activities is that I *am* careful, and I'm prudent and watchful, with perhaps a tinge of passion and impulsiveness thrown in on occasion. I wish I were more reckless and outspoken. I wish my words of resistance would flow easily from my mouth in screams and songs and rage, filling the canyons and arroyos.

There are many heroes in the borderlands of southern Arizona. Even though our present government may have lost its humanity, most of our people have not. My neighbors and friends have helped migrants lost in the desert, and many have rendered assistance far more effectively than I. While President Trump pledges to expel the "bad hombres," there are networks of sanctuary and refuge that operate quietly and effectively every day. People seek refuge in churches, houses, sheds, and barns. While Congress debates how best to confront the eleven million undocumented people residing in our country, thankfully the people of the borderlands reach out to help the huddled masses in spite of the endless and mean-spirited chatter in the halls of Congress.

I've pondered how I have come to this place in my life. The racism present in my childhood and adolescence was no small thing. My father taught me to fear and avoid people of color. The lessons around the dinner table were this: White people are better than people of color. It was a message of white superiority. Dad also taught us to revere the written word. We were encouraged to read, and to talk about the ideas that appeared on the page. Reading books that refuted my father's dinner table lectures kept my own mind in a state of constant questioning.

My mother quietly enabled my father's beliefs about race, class, ethnicity. She was the peace-maker and lived her convictions of acceptance and diversity without talking about them. She kept the family together, and I marvel how she did this. I never really knew what my mother believed until after my father died. Then I watched as she volunteered at a local nonprofit organization for abused and neglected children. I watched as she accepted and celebrated the ideas and vicissitudes of her children and grandchildren. She flourished. Their marriage was complex and passionate and confounding.

I never quite bought into the conversations around the dinner table. Usually my dad had too much to drink when the vitriol poured out, and mom focused on dad, placating his tirades as best she could. Meanwhile, we three kids sat and listened and did our best to figure out our own survival strategies. I never doubted that my parents loved all of us dearly. But it was Chicago, the 1940s, and the culture of white supremacy was rampant in my South Side neighborhood.

The tragedy of Emmett Till has stuck with me throughout my life. I think it provoked a level of empathy in my parents as well, as they were troubled that a young boy could meet an untimely demise at the hands of crazed white men in the Deep South.

And Emmett was a Chicago boy. I'm grateful that we discussed Emmett at the dinner table. The lesson I remember, however, was one of caution. Don't even try to get involved with people of color. They are different, the "other." Bad things will happen if you cross color lines, and your family will probably disown you. Again, I never quite accepted the family's rule book about race and ethnicity. How can you vilify an entire group of people when you've never talked to them?

The difficulties and struggles with our first-born, our daughter, affected me in ways I still haven't quite figured out. December is a month I want to spend close to home. I'm vulnerable, weepy, happy and full of the spirit of babies and music and sweet Jesus in the manger. But when Juan Carlos collapsed on our doorstep, he threw me into a tailspin. Feeling vulnerable and panicked and terrified, I did the best I could. He is my Guatemalan son, and I feel like part of his growing family.

It seems that the most difficult times in my life are the ones that give me the most strength. Those experiences propel me forward and give me juice. I love the moments when I have no fear.

And yet here's a confession: Whenever I hear the dogs barking and raising Cain in the darkness outside our home, I cringe. There are days and nights when I don't want to deal with the stranger, the messiness of caring for another human being in need, standing at my door.

One time Juan Carlos phoned and our dogs were barking nonstop at something outside the door. "You better go check what the dogs are barking at," J.C. said, laughing. "It could be another lost *migrante.*" It was the laughter of a shared experience, and he couldn't stop chuckling about it all.

Thankfully I listened to my better angels when attending to the needs of Juan Carlos on that solstice eve several years ago. He challenged my fears and competency as a human being and a caretaker. We bumbled through those days together, and the bonds of trust grew stronger as a result of our inadequacies. I believe that both my husband and I are better people for it.

THIRTY-FOUR

Happy New Year

New Year's Day, 2018
Margarita

Juan Carlos left some messages on my cell phone over the past two days. Finally I call him back. The connection is crackling and our cell phones are continually breaking up. Every second or third word is lost. I can't figure out how to say the phone reception is "breaking up" in Spanish, and so we stumble along trying to communicate the simplest thoughts. As he walks up the street in his tiny village in Guatemala, Juan Carlos's voice finally comes through. He's figured out the best spot for our phone conversation—on a rock where he sits at the side of a dusty road.

"My cow has died and so has the newborn calf. The cow doctor wants too much money for medicines, and when I pay it, the cow dies anyway!" He is venting, and telling me a long, convoluted story about his cow.

I take a deep breath, thinking that my friend needs some cash to keep his business afloat. But I am wrong.

Instead he gives me my first gift of the new year.

"Margarita, I have never been happier than I am at this very moment."

"Really?" Have I gotten lost in translation again?

"Even though my cow died, I am a happy man. My life is good."

He has two jobs. His family is healthy, his children are happy, and he is in the middle of preparing a special dinner for this New Year's Day. There are always dogs barking, children shrieking, a parrot squawking, and cars honking. He tells me he has everything he needs to be happy today. I can barely hear him, but his words touch my heart.

After many wishes of health and prosperity for the new year and many thank-you's for being his friend, we hang up. I've spent countless moments wondering where all of this was going. What were my financial contributions and phone calls each month really accomplishing? What was the hook that kept me tethered to this man in Guatemala?

Every once in a while we encounter someone who bonds with us on a soul level, inexplicably and persistently. My odyssey with Juan Carlos taught me a few things. There is no "other." It's all us. I learned what I'm made of and what I'm not. And what I want to become.

THIRTY-FIVE

Firebird

A FINCH SLAMMED into my window the other day and lay in a feathery lump in the sun on the patio, stunning itself into bird oblivion. Where the bird had smashed into the glass, there was a feathery imprint that looked like a celestial ghost. The critter wanted in, a stranger at my window.

The television was on, and CNN was in a mood of outrage and head-shaking disbelief. President Trump had just described Haiti, El Salvador and Africa as "shit-hole countries," and he wanted to shut the door on any immigrants or refugees who claimed these lands as their country of origin.

I looked out at the crimson-breasted house finch lying on the patio. The bird looked dead. With a paper towel in hand, I carefully placed the inert bird on the patio table so the neighboring cats and fire ants wouldn't have their way with the little fluff ball. I'll bury it later.

Watching the uproar on the TV about Trump's "shit-hole" reference to hundreds of millions of people, I felt dead, like the bird on my table. Dead tired. The idea that people from poor countries are somehow lesser human beings is abhorrent to me. I hate the words spouting from the president's mouth.

Outside, I saw the little concussed bird quiver, and then I noticed that it had pooped on my checkered tablecloth. It was alive. Struggling to stand, it began shaking its wings furiously, and then its whole body. It was shaking itself awake. Half hopping and falling off the table, it landed on the patio bricks and lurched in circles like a drunken sailor. In a Saint Vitus' dance of fits and starts, the little bird shook its way back to life. After thirty minutes, it was gone, having risen from the dead. A Lazarus bird.

I decided I needed to shake it up a little myself and put on Stravinsky's "Firebird Suite." There's a great timpani part at the end that jolts you like a lightning bolt. It always wakes up a sleepy audience. I love pounding out that rhythm and have done so in many orchestras and bands over the years.

Listening to the music, I imagined a firebird dancing around my living room. I had just seen it, or something like it, on my patio. And so I danced around too, shaking my arms and booty like my feathered friend on the patio. The dog joined me, looking at me like I was a little nuts. We danced together. For the first time in a long while, I felt connected to my body, my mind, my soul. In a way, I rose from the ashes. The incessant rhythms of Stravinsky kept me moving, and the improvisation of my life seemed to make more sense as I bounced around with a crazy grin on my face.

BIBLIOGRAPHY

Bowden, Charles, *Some Of the Dead Are Still Breathing*. New York: Houghton Mifflin Harcourt, 2009.

Chapman, Peter, *Bananas: How the United Fruit Company Shaped the World*. New York: Canongate, 2007.

Fried, Jonathan L., Marvin E. Gettleman, Deborah T. Levenson, Nancy Peckenham, ed., *Guatemala in Rebellion: Unfinished History*. New York: Grove Press, Inc., 1983.

Garrison, Thomas, George Black, Milton Jamail, and Norma Stoltz Chinchilla, *Guatemala*. New York: Monthly Review Press, 1984.

McClintock, Michael, *The American Connection, Volume Two*. London: Zed Books Ltd., 1985.

Schlesinger, Stephen and Stephen Kinzer, *Bitter Fruit*. Garden City, New York: Anchor Books, Anchor Press/Doubleday, 1983.

Shapiro, Michael, *Guatemala, A Journey through the Land of the Maya*. Monte Rio, California: Purple Moon Publications, 2008.

BIG THANKS

A FEW THINGS need to be shouted from the rooftops: The real work in the borderlands is something that one does not do alone. Many kind, generous people patiently listened to my frustrations and teeth-gnashing during the writing of this memoir. My wild women friends of Tubac and Green Valley offered me their company, their margaritas, and their hearts.

I could not have written this book without the help of Jerry Ervin, my editor and best friend. He was able to poke holes in whatever I was saying, but then was kind enough to point me in the direction of light and clarity. I owe a thank-you to Bette Ervin for helping me with translations of letters and documents.

Sister Judy and the Sisters of Notre Dame in Douglas, Arizona, have been my spiritual guides and inspiration. Their activism pulled me out of my chair and my internal dialogue with NPR and The New York Times, and propelled me into the real world of the borderlands. Plus the homemade bread and wine have been my holy communion with these angels of Douglas and Agua Prieta.

I owe a lot of gratitude to our son, Sage Weil, who offered me refuge and unconditional support during my move to Tubac. I also want to give a shout-out to Cheyenne Weil, our daughter, who never stopped believing that what I did was the right thing to do, even though *I* had my doubts. The grandchildren—Riley, Damon, Kiera and Ronin—kept me focused on the essentials: collecting rocks in the desert, building boats with twigs at Patagonia Lake, singing songs by the piano.

I am thankful for the partnership and long history of desert life with *mi esposo,* Lester Weil.

Finally, I am indebted to Jake, our dog, who always put his paw on my leg when he knew I needed to push my chair away from the computer screen and take a walk in the sun.

ABOUT

====> • <====

the Author

PEG BOWDEN (R.N., M.S.) is a retired public health nurse who lives in southern Arizona near the U.S./Mexico border. She is a humanitarian aid worker with the Green Valley/Sahuarita Samaritans, and volunteers weekly with the migrant population at *el comedor*, a place of refuge in Nogales, Sonora. A musician and artist, Peg pounds the timpani in the Green Valley Concert Band, and paints watercolors of her beloved desert. She lives with her husband, Lester Weil, a couple of dogs, a feral cat, and a lot of open range cattle.

ALSO BY

Peg Bowden

Accolades for
A Land of Hard Edges

Peg Bowden breathes life into crucial border issues so often lost in polemic. She sits us down to lunch with desperate, destitute Mexicans, our neighbors.

Mort Rosenblum, reporter, author, educator

While U.S. migrant policy limps on bleeding feet and ignores its own hungers, a million uprooted poor huddle along our southwestern border. Instead of proverbial loaves and fishes, now it's grandmothers handing out burritos and hot coffee. Come spend a day with Bowden in the soup kitchen called *el comedor.* Filled with courage and compassion, this uplifting book is the best on the human side of the immigration equation that I've yet read.

Bill Broyles, writer, educator, author of *Sunshot: Peril and Wonder in the Gran Desierto*

The stories Bowden tells are often gut-wrenching, but she gives us hope in a world of angry political rhetoric in the resilience of the human spirit and the healing power of good works.

Bruce J. Dinges, Ph.D., author, retired editor of
The Journal of Arizona History.

Peg's experiences on the border not only reflect her dedication to helping others, but lend themselves to her thoughtful and analytic approach to social issues. *A Land of Hard Edges* provides a very insightful yet informative approach to understanding the issues around immigration.

Rosalie Caffrey, Ph.D., Professor Emeritus,
Oregon Health and Sciences University